FUMBLES, STUMBLES, AND GRUMBLES

FUMBLES, STUMBLES, AND GRUMBLES

Essays on the Art of Haphazard Living

ANNE VALENTINE

Words and Photos by Anne Valentine

LUCID MOON

PUBLISHING

Published by Lucid Moon Publishing

For information contact: av.valentine@gmail.com

Book cover and interior design by Anne Valentine
and Francine Platt of Eden Graphics, Inc.

Paperback ISBN 979-8-89454-087-0

eBook ISBN 979-8-89454-088-7

Library of Congress Control Number: 2024904696

Manufactured in the United States of America

First Edition

10 9 8 7 6 5 4 3 2 1

CONTENTS

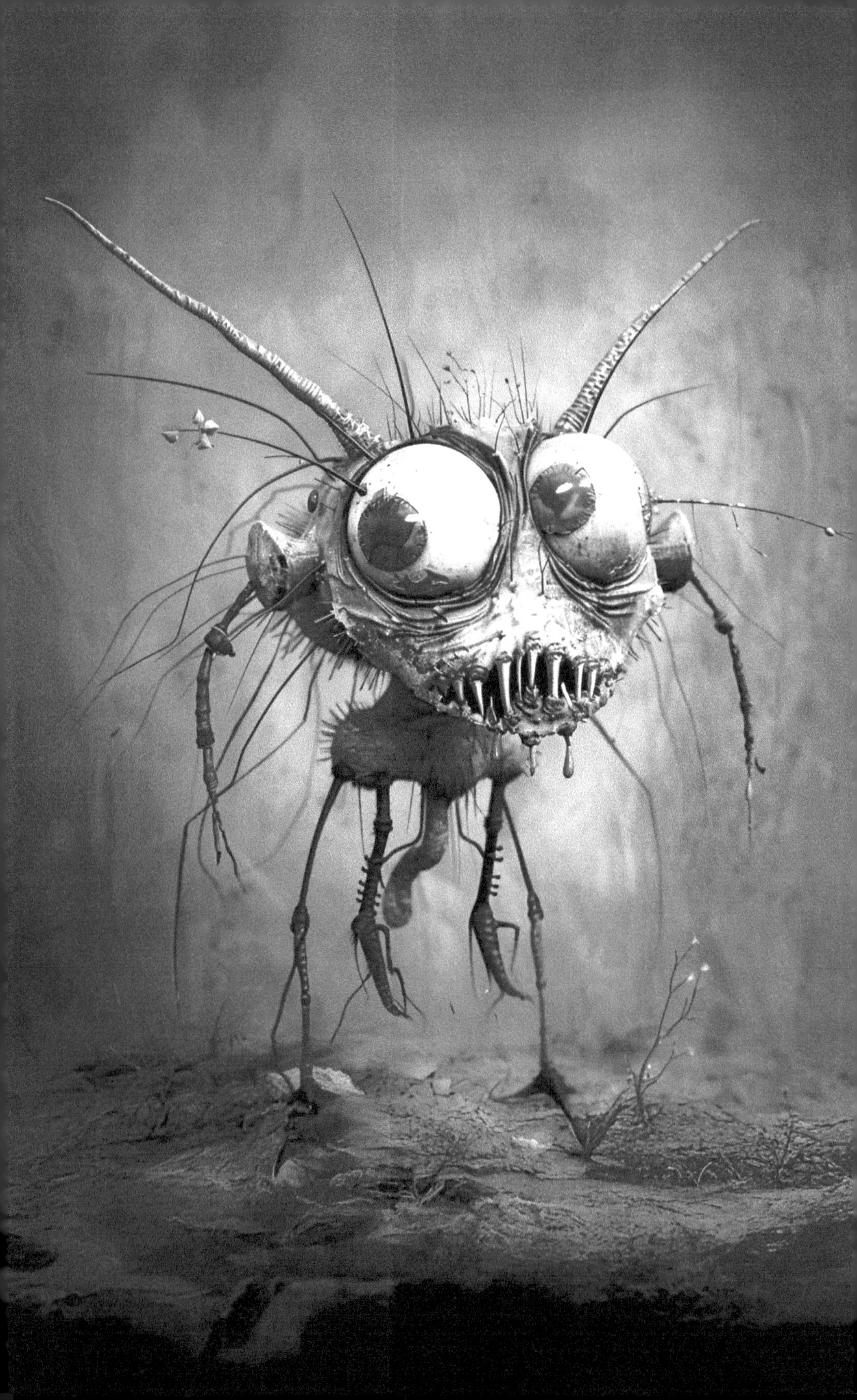

MENACE

Today, I had a *moment*…and there were witnesses. There were also victims.

I was standing in line to get some lunch when it occurred to me I was getting takeout, so I told the guy behind me, "I'll be right back," and sped off to trade in my plate for a takeout container. When I returned, two women stood in my place. Confused, but giving them the benefit of the doubt and thinking maybe they had permission to cut in line, I asked the guy holding my place if he knew why they were there. He just shrugged.

Instantly, my hackles raised. Line jumpers are the worst! Before I knew it, I was salivating, and demanding an explanation.

No matter how they spun it, their excuse for cutting the line made no sense. Eventually, they apologized, and went to the back of the line, which was, admittedly, quite short.

When it was my turn at the counter, I placed my order, but had to wait for the employee to fill my container. With the line being as short as it was, and with how quickly it was moving, the line jumpers ended up right next to me. Since I was still waiting for my meal, I decided to let them go ahead. It wasn't so much kindness as it was calculation on my part. After all, I figured I had to do something to offset my previous Pavlovian reaction towards them.

You see, I was born overseas in a country that was once a British Crown Colony. Being fully immersed in English culture, I was polite, had a proper British accent, and had impeccable manners. All that came with me when we moved back to the States, and to this day, I still have the expectation of British civility.

I can use the correct spoon, identify different wine/cordial glasses, and wait for staff to put the napkin in my lap. Indeed, I can certainly keep up with some of the most muckety mucks, but damn, sometimes I just don't know how to deal with people and let the little things slide. Waiting your turn in line definitely falls under the category of good manners. So, this afternoon, my rigid ideas of proper public manners had caused enough embarrassment, and I didn't want to hold up the line.

I've spent the better part of the last twenty years learning to be gracious, embrace humanity, meet life on life's terms, and identify my patterns. Despite all of that, when my amygdala gets hijacked, there is a creature, a little demon, a menace inside my soul that refuses to be corralled. She is one of several, and is more displeased and antsy because she has seen the light of day less and less over those twenty years, and needs retribution. When Menace surfaces these days, there's chaos-a-comin'!

Today, in response to the line jumpers, she appeared in a flash and emphatically hissed in my ear, *DID. YOU. SEE. THAT?* And in a nanosecond, I was offended, indignant, posturing, and making an ass out of myself, while Menace quietly stepped back into the shadows, satisfied with the toll I just paid for not letting her out to play, and satisfied with the mayhem I created.

Meanwhile, at the end of the line, still waiting for my to-go container, I started beating myself up like Dobby the house elf of Harry Potter fame. The self-flagellation was mind-numbingly overdone, but I couldn't stop. Had I a rosary available for my Catholic half and my Star of David for my Jewish half, there would have been guilt carnage.

To top it all off, I had a hard time enjoying my lunch, the very one I just paid for in multiple currencies.

SWEET GIRL №1

You are growing,
Faster now than ever,
And it hurts.
Your heart aches.
Your bones ache.
Your conscience aches.
You are faced with decisions
That now affect others,
And that is confusing.
The world is confusing.
People are confusing.
Love is confusing.
But I know you…
I know your heart,
I know your burgeoning light.
You are being shaped and molded.
It is not easy; it hurts,
But you are to be the best "you" we can make—
Like shaping wood or metal.
It, like you, resists and fights.
It, like you, bends and yields.
There is resistance and pain,
There is light and beauty,
There is strength that, in time, does emerge.
You will be tempted; you will be teased.
Never let that light go out.
That will be the hardest thing you do.

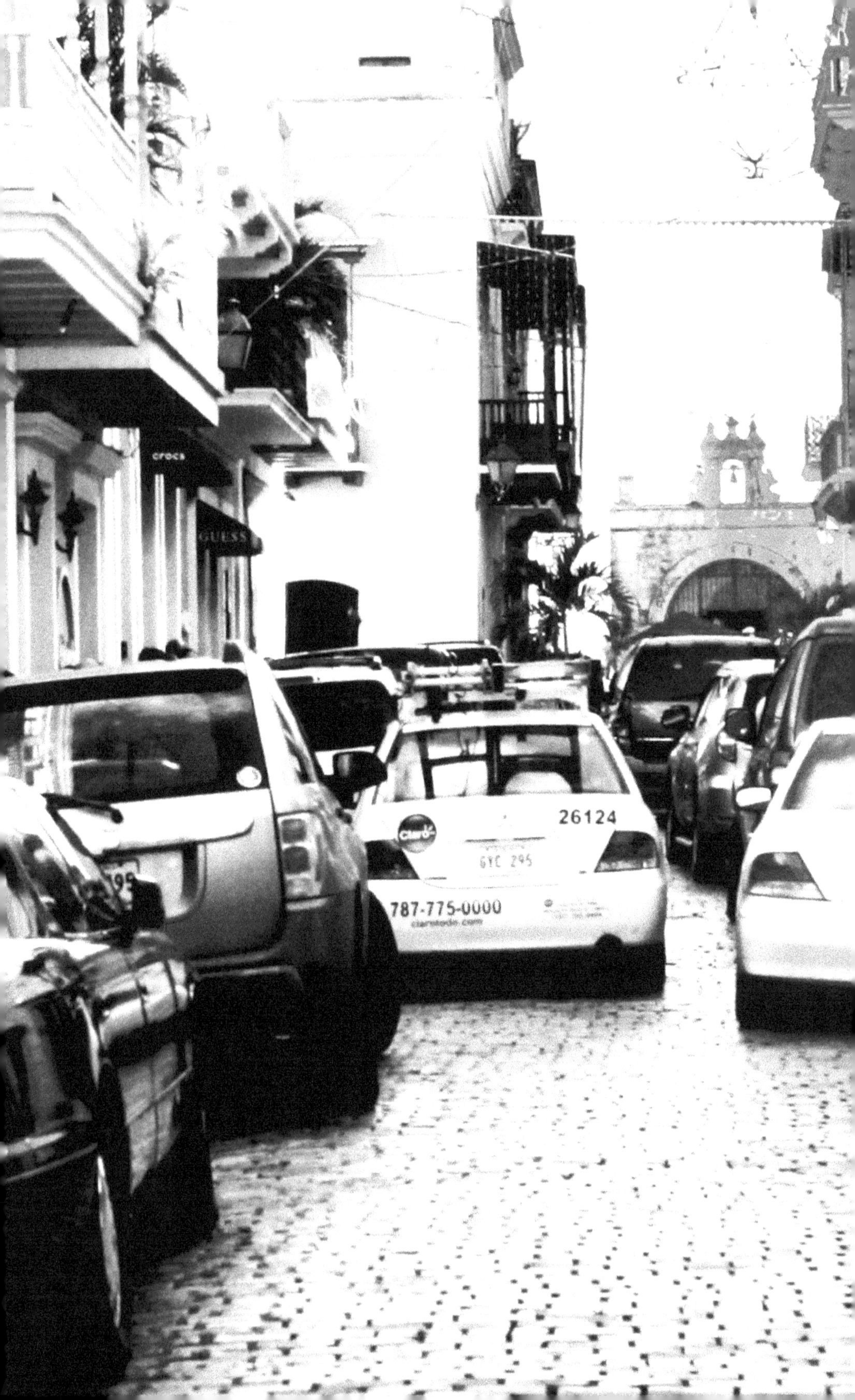
crocs
GUESS
Claro
787-775-0000
clarotodo.com
26124
GYC 295

THE F WORD

My dad's brother told his kids there were two words in the English language he never wanted to hear uttered from their mouths. Both words began with the letter *F*. Fully expecting my silent generation uncle to say the worst of the two *F*-words was *f**k*, I was quite taken aback when he said the most heinous of the two was *fair*. I was speechless, but the gears in my brain kicked into high. That was the first time I ever considered *fair* to be a four-letter word.

One of several *modus operandi* that run me is *fair or not fair*. My parents, in contrast to my aunt and uncle, lived their lives making sure that our family life was fair. If I got a present that cost less than my sister's, Mom and Dad gave me the difference in cash. Same for her. There were many birthdays and Christmases I'd get a handful of change to make up any difference in the cost of our gifts.

It took a while before I realized the gift the relationship failures were

While my mother was versed in many things, vocabulary was her jam. No kid of hers would show her ignorance through poor vocabulary and grammar by default, because what's the point of showing off worthy vocabulary if your grammar sucks? We were never allowed to swear, much less drop the F-bomb.

And if we did, we bypassed the cuss bucket, which already contained so much of my hard-earned allowance, and went straight to the bar of soap with which "to wash out your filthy mouth." So another M.O. is an ear for bad grammar and vocabulary. I will notice incorrect use of the English language faster than I notice the good use of it. That should be ordinary. At least in my world.

Another *F*-word to add to this short but potent list is *failure*. I have gotten so wadded up when striking out at a game or worse, being the reason my team lost the game. Some of my biggest failures have been in relationships. They have also been some of my most painful failures. The pain is exponential when heartbreak is attached. It took a while before I realized the gift the relationship failures were. I learned what I was willing to put up with and what I wasn't. My deal-breaker list got longer and longer over the years with each failed relationship. Of course, if I was the one who got dumped, it was *never* fair, and I left in a wake of F-bombs to begin again.

SWEET GIRL №2

Sweet girl,

You played your heart out

And you didn't win.

And that really is okay.

We teach you it is all about the prize

But that is a lie.

It is a heartbreaking lie.

What matters most is your heart.

The heart you exhausted to do your best;

The heart you exposed in vulnerable agony;

The heart you were willing to let break.

A winning spirit always prevails;

Triumph or defeat.

Lose graciously.

Hold your head high for a battle well fought.

Win humbly.

Praise your opponent for a battle well fought.

There is no prize for lacing up, showing up.

There is no prize for fighting a good fight.

The prize is in the mirror, at the end

When you can say "I done good!!"

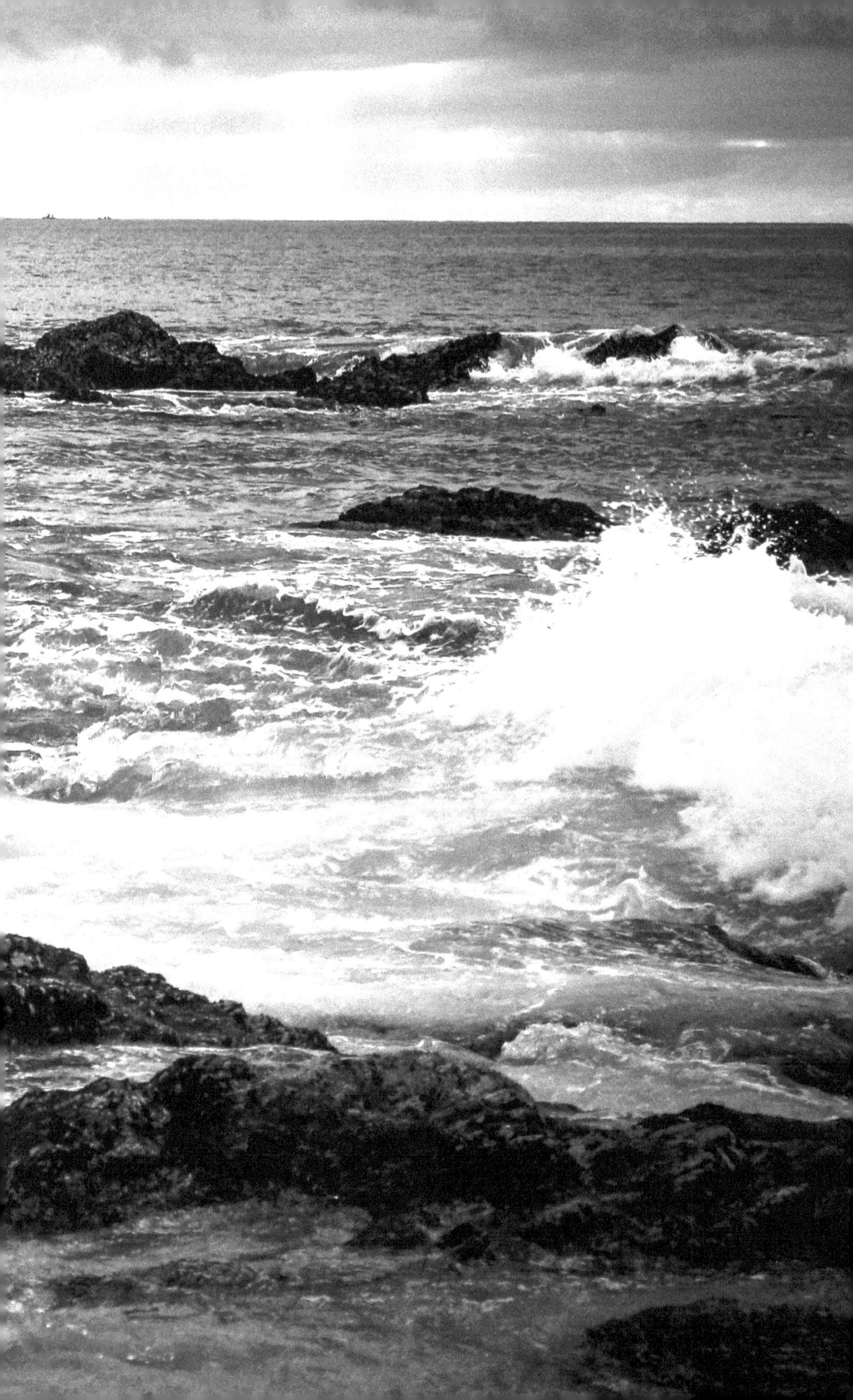

COMFY

The fabric is more of a mustard yellow than gold. The cuffs are frayed and coming off the body, the hem has split, and there are so many random little holes, it looks more like a pair of fishnet stockings than the beloved sweater it is, but that's another topic for a different day.

It is my favorite old sweatshirt, and it's the colors of the Green Bay Packers. Given it came from Wisconsin, it's rather fitting. "UP NORTH Wisconsin" is stitched in green lettering across the front of the gold fabric. It is a souvenir gift from my sister, who got it while on a summer trip to visit her childhood BFF in . . . wait for it . . . Up-North Wisconsin.

One evening, after the summer sun descended into the Northwoods darkness, a chill came over the night. My sister pulled the brand-new sweatshirt over her head, leaving the tags still attached to the cuff. She caught all kinds of grief from the collection of cheese-heads there that evening. All those native Wisconsinites made fun of their prodigal daughter for being cold on a late summer evening in The Dairy State.

You have to know, we had been living in Texas for the better part of forty years and had gotten quite accustomed to the heat of hell unleashed on us every July and August. Of all the places we lived, Texas is the longest. It is not my favorite, but I am the most comfortable here.

The sweatshirt—two sizes too big—swallowed her up like a

little girl in her daddy's shirt, but she wore it anyway. My sister bundled up in that sweatshirt while everyone else was in shorts and t-shirts.

Some twenty years later, I still have that old sweatshirt despite being threadbare. It has been tossed in corners, in the way back of my car, and in the very back of the closet. It's been spit up on, puked on, and cried on. It stretched when I gained weight and shrank too many times to count when I had to wash it in extra-hot water. To look at it, you would think it should have gone in the rubbish long ago. In a culture where things are replaced before the shine is off, I should have replaced it three times over. But there is something in this old sweatshirt that cannot be replaced. To anyone else, it is a ratty old piece of clothing, not even fit for the second-hand store; rags, perhaps, but not much more. Over the years it has given me warmth, comfort, and a feeling of being taken care of by my little sister. To me, it is priceless.

Such is a person's life, worn and frayed, patched up and back on the shelf to be used over and over again.

This is my legacy sweatshirt.

I can only hope my life is as rich and worn, and feels as safe and as comfortable to the ones I love.

I DON'T DISAGREE

My mom was a grammar snob. She was also a pain about manners. We were not allowed to swear, and when we did, she hissed, "I taught you better than that." And she did! I think her biggest thing was "Can I?" Like, "Can I go to the movies with Susie?" She would *always* say, "I don't know, can you?"

I'd scrunch up my face at her, and she just stared back at me, until I said, "May I?"

"Yes, you may." And that was that. Off I ran to wherever.

One of my biggest joys in life was listening to my mom cuss like a sailor when she got older. She'd drop the F-bomb, the one I'm still not allowed to say.

I'd say "Mooommm!" in that long, punctuated, drawn-out kinda way we use when we are not happy with somebody.

Her reply? "Weeellllll?"

My paternal grandmother was even worse. We could not say back and forth: it had to be forth and back or to and fro because it was logically more correct.

Ask me why. . . ?

Please. Come on. Ask.

Not only was it logistically correct, but she preferred the *tintinnabulation* of it. In non-grammar-snob speak, she liked the way it sounded better. While the rest of the world puts their shoes and socks on, we put our socks and shoes on: though not common, it is technically correct.

Don't get me started about ending a sentence with a preposition! If you ask me, "Where are you at?" I will always reply, "Behind the at." In my opinion, irregardless is repetitive and unnecessary and usually spoken by some poor unsuspecting soul who did not have grammar snobs as parents.

But let's talk about the expression "I don't disagree" in all of its poor grammar glory. Double negatives were my dad's personal nemesis. I just love this one because I can say it, and it lulls the other person into thinking I agree with them in a very noncommittal, back door, escape hatch kinda way. While I don't disagree, I am not quite agreeing either. I am covertly pleading the metaphorical fifth, letting the other person think I agree, and if pressed I can always say, "That's not what I said."

The English language is a dynamic and ever-changing thing. We say things today that would have shocked the sensibilities of the boldest Puritan years ago. *Shoot* (as in, "Oh, shoot," not as in "shoot a gun") used to be profane. I will continue to keep my prepositions off the end of my sentences and just keep regard to the suffix only, as in regard-*less*. No *ir*-regardless for me. Ever.

But I will always love me some "don't disagree."

SWEET GIRL №3

Sweet girl,

It gets better.

Not today.

Not tomorrow.

But when you don't notice,

When you think it's impossible,

The hurt retreats

The floodwaters recede.

And what's left behind

Is the debris and memory

Of an imperfect life.

A life uniquely human.

And when enough days go by

And the flood is gone

And you've picked through the debris,

What remains are the pieces,

Of a life, uniquely, human.

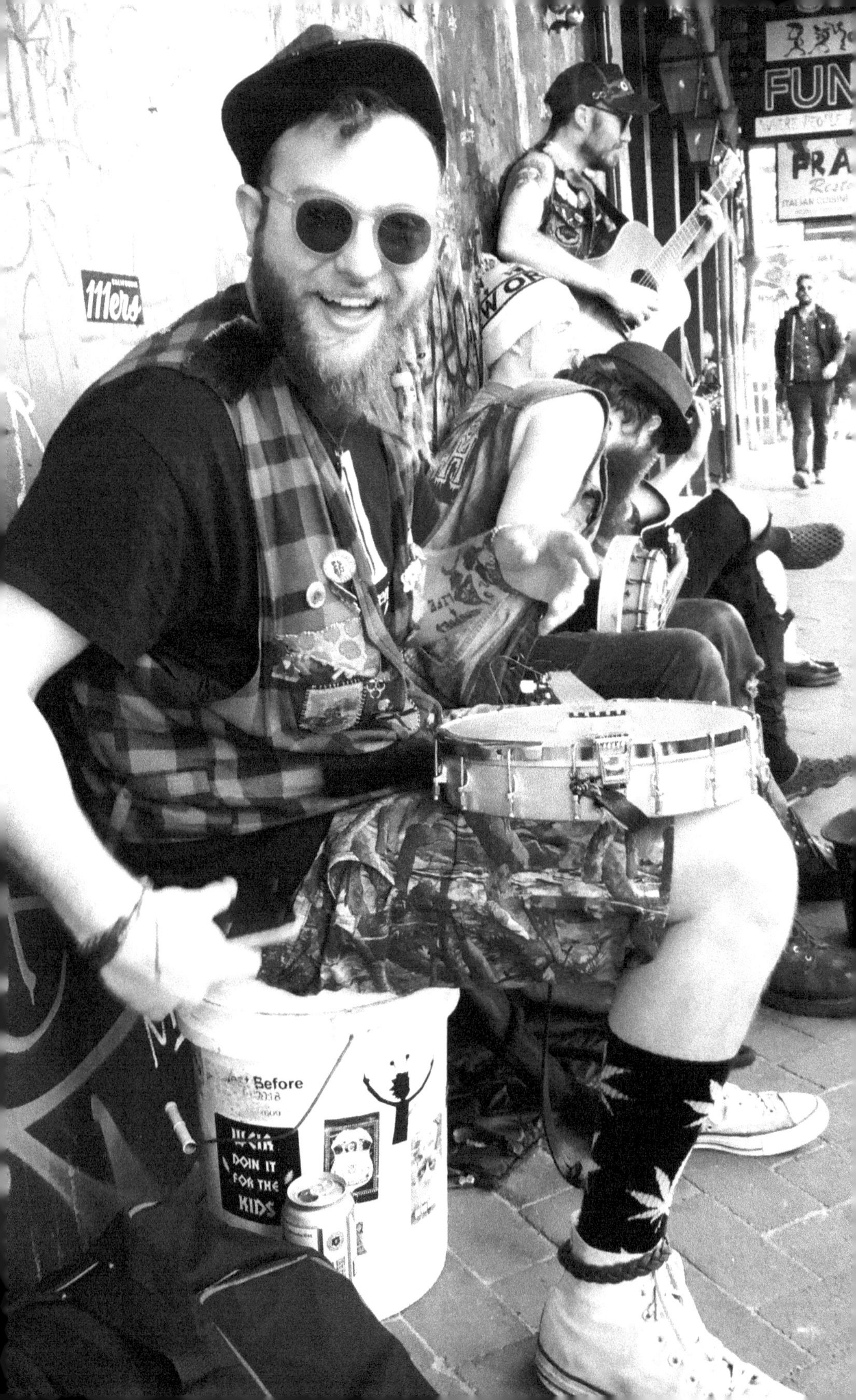
111ers
FUN
PRA
Best Before
DOIN IT
FOR THE
KIDS

NOT SO FATAL FLAWS

We all want the perfect job, perfect relationship, perfect body. Look around. We are bombarded with cures and fixes for all of our flaws. There are pills, injections, implants, removals, meal replacements, diets galore, self-help, self-reliance, coaches, consultants, transformation, transcendentalism, transcontinental (kidding), info-mercials, google for everything, psychology, philosophy, ontology, technology, and any number of other *ologies* to make the imper-fect perfect. And over the years, I have bought, subscribed, popped, injected, read, watched, followed, ate, not ate, studied, thought, fought, listened, and cried seeking perfection. The funny thing is, in seeking that perfection, it all became a part of the journey. And that's what I forgot; perfection is a journey, not a destination.

There is a difference in the feel, a difference in my experience of a perfect piece of art spit out by a machine versus something that is an intentional creation, a perfectly imperfect human endeavor.

I work mind-numbingly, crazy-makingly, exhaustingly hard to produce perfect pieces of art. Here too, I forget that what gets accomplished is really about the journey, not the end result. There is no fun, no soul in that kind of work. In that place, I get frustrated, angry, resentful, even hateful. Whether the art is my job, my body, my relationship, or my actual works of art, I want the soul of it first and foremost. I don't want any of it to be seen as perfect. I'd rather it be seen as soulful.

There is a difference in the feel, a difference in my experience of a perfect piece of art spit out by a machine versus something that is an intentional creation, a perfectly imperfect human endeavor. I believe our souls are in those imperfections, those flaws. I want the piece of art into which someone has poured her heart and soul; that which is the end result of a personal journey, the degree to which I will probably never know other than to know there is one. I want the finished work that is a result of the journey and where that journey is reflected back.

I want a creation that is inherently flawed and presumed perfect, where beauty is in the flaws and perfection in the eye of the beholder. I want that which is the result of trial and error, the result of starting over, the result of forgiveness.

BANNED

Why, exactly, are we still banning books? Banning books, like all the ill–conceived isms, should be a thing of the past. Unfortunately, it seems we added a few more to the list like xenophobia, Islamophobia, and ableism to name a few. Anyway, I looked up various lists of banned books. I've already read many of them, so it seems crazy to ban them now. Now I'm going to read the others!

Ya know, if you tell a kid "no," it's like an open–door invitation to them. Perhaps not a literal open door so much, but a door through which they will find their way. They will go to great lengths and bend all kinds of rules just because they aren't supposed to. "No" is a teenage anthem, the anti-authoritarian fuel to their "F you, nobody gets me" angst.

The chorus of "no's" became her gasoline-fueled fight song and all her parents did with each "no" was hand her a match.

My sister dated a guy my parents did not like at all. They could not even generate the graciousness to accept him as a living, breathing soul just sharing space on the planet. They made so much noise about him and were so vocal about their dislike and disapproval of him that it turbo-charged my sister into overdrive and into his arms faster than they could say, "He's not good for you."

A friend grew up with a glass bookcase loaded with books

her parents didn't want her to read. They were very vocal about their daughter having a relationship with the books in that case. The chorus of "no's" became her gasoline-fueled fight song, and all her parents did with each "no" was hand her a match. What started out as no interest became a single–cell curiosity. As with evolution, this single cell took on a life all its own. Zero interest became an "I wonder. . ." which became "what if . . ." which became "I want to—I'm going to. . ." which ultimately became, "I am reading those books!"

And then, in the seconds before her parents could say "no," she was consumed by a fire where once there was nothing combustible; nothing with which to even catch a spark. Sometimes "no" is all it takes for otherwise inert, stable, unsuspecting ingredients to go BOOM. She read almost all of the books in the cabinet before she got busted. The book with which she got caught? *Gone With the Wind.*

So, okay then, ban away if you must.

THE ROAD NOT TRAVELED

Robert Frost wrote about a road in the woods that split. He stood at their juncture deciding which one to take and at the same time, lamenting the one not taken. Ultimately, he felt better for having chosen the road less traveled. There are many metaphors that can be applied to roads, paths, crossroads, intersections, going fast, going slow, going back again, and the like, but this is not about any of that.

Many times I find myself at points in my life, wondering, *How did I get here?* Not the physical here, but the emotional here. Though the physical here is often a part of the emotional here. Like right here, right now. It's not a good or a bad thing, it's just a thing. I don't think about all the decisions made or not made, all the things I did or didn't do, or everything I said or didn't say to get me to this point.

Until I do think about it

Remember when we were kids going on a family vacation? My family piled into the old station wagon with faux wood panels on the outside, and within an hour my sister and I were asleep. We woke up moments before we arrived and wondered how we got there, and more importantly, how we got there so fast. So today, I look back on my life—the Cliff Notes version, not the unabridged version, and I really do wonder how I got here so fast.

It seems I've been rather unintentional about my life in general. There are things I have been very intentional about, like school, but more often than not, it is as if I came upon different points in time in complete randomness and by accident. The truth is, I dare say we, because I don't think I'm the only one; I think we slept through the trip.

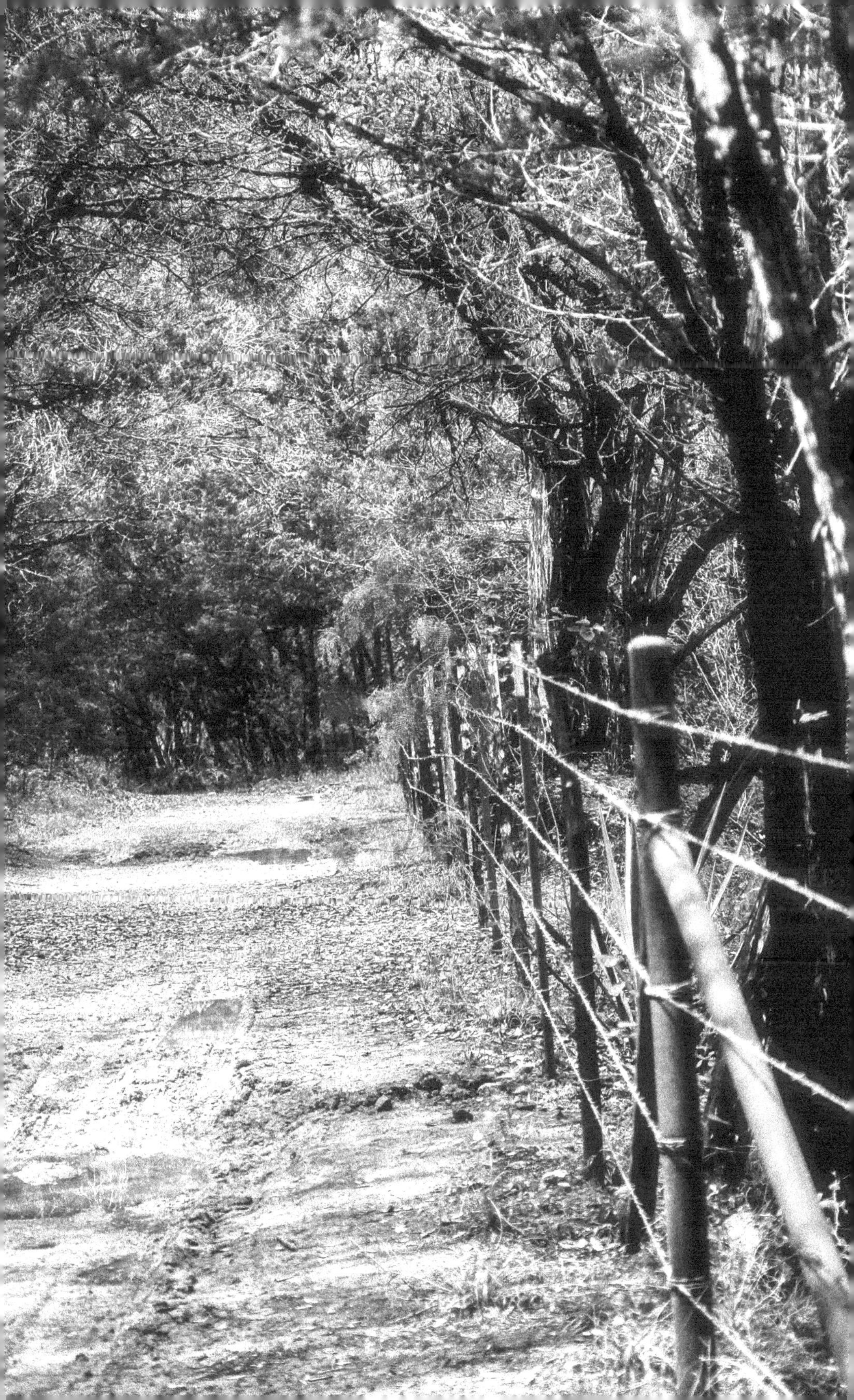

BEHOLD

Behold your words.
They are the building blocks
Of wishes, dreams, and desires.
Carefully crafted mantras
With intention and purpose,
Then set upon the winds.
To the ears of heaven they are sent
And lay the foundation for futures
Of love and hope and promise.
Words are the beacon
That sets a direction
And echoes a destination.
They are the verbal embrace,
The confidence we gift,
And the blessings we bestow.

BEWARE

Beware your words
They are tools of devastation
Destroying lives, hopes, and ambitions
Words, misguided and thrown to the ethers
With malintent and ill will:
Meant to cover a wide swath
They go straight to the heart of hell
Fueled by the furies
Where passage is granted
At a cost not easily afforded
Unbridled upon the hearts of the intended
And often bequeathed to the next generation
They are the verbal sword
The pain we inflict;
The damage we leave behind

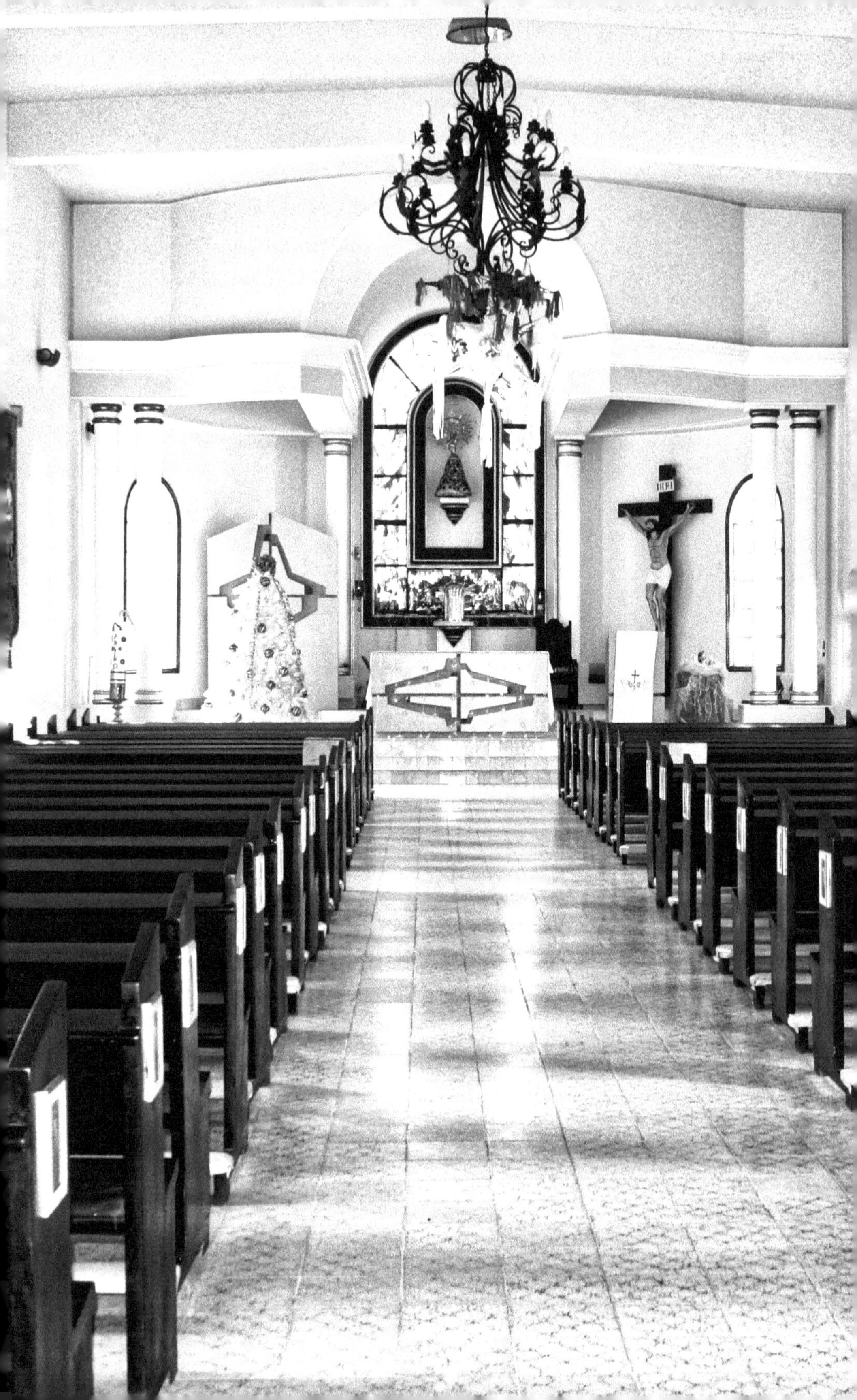

THERE BUT . . .

The next couple of pages come with this warning: this may be considered inflammatory by some, and it may piss off the rest, and maybe that's a good thing. As such, it sounds a bit sermon-y, all because I watched the news and got pissed off myself.

The story on the news was about a bunch of middle-aged white guys complaining. They felt left out because they did not have their own parade and were going to create one. With everything going on in the world, THIS made the national news and it really, really, really (too many reallys?) got my ire! So, hold on to your hats—baseball, cowboy, or otherwise—and read on with an open mind and a whole lotta love. Ready?

There is a weight, a heaviness to the goings-on of today that burdens even the strongest of shoulders. No matter the side of the aisle or tracks you're on or the size of your bank account, as people of America, our motto ought to be, "There but for the grace of God, go I." If the word *God* trips you up, then insert whatever works for you. And if you are going to argue agnosticism and atheism with me, my reply is this: 1. This is not about that. 2. YOU KNOW WHAT I MEAN!

If you have never had to worry about your son surviving past twenty-five, you don't get your own parade. If you don't worry about being deported or getting beat up or killed because you feel like you were born the wrong gender, you do not get your own parade. If you don't worry about being thrown into jail at the whim of another, getting groped or worse, raped just because you are "the fairer sex," have to fight for the same wages as your coworkers or fight to be considered equal, You. Do. Not. Get. Your. Own. Parade. All lives matter, and if you never felt like yours didn't, you do not get a parade.

I doubt that Black Lives Matter, Gay Pride, or The Women's March does any parade, any celebration, at the expense of another. These celebrations are born from the outer rims of society where inequality and marginalization are the norm. You have to ache to want to belong, to be a part of, and to be considered equal. You have to want for belonging from a place where there is no acceptance and be willing to create that acceptance. You have to dig deep and look hard for that beacon of acceptance, and when those doors open, you know you are home. You cannot want for something because someone else has it and you don't, not this time.

So step outside, look around, and be grateful you don't get a parade. Say to yourself, *There, but for the grace of God, go I.* My goal is to live a life where no parade is needed or wanted.

I do get one parade, and I am so very happy it's just the one.

THAT PERSON

Early in the work morning I joined two of my coworkers who were sitting at a workstation with a long line of unoccupied computers. Before sitting, I reached into my pocket, and when I did, I sustained an injury. I got a deep paper cut along the entire width of my fingertip from a paper I had folded and pocketed earlier. It was the middle finger of my right hand. The very finger I use to flip the bird. In my pain and exasperation, I declared, after a succession of words inappropriate for the workplace, "Dammit, this is my typing finger!"

One of my coworkers cocked her head and, with a very puzzled look on her face, said, "Your typing finger . . . ?" She and I have only been working together for about two years.

The other coworker and I have worked together for about ten years. So she replied saying, "Don't even try to figure it out—it's just Anne."

We all got a good chuckle and went about our business, but I was left with the nagging question, *what does she mean, "Just Anne?"* I'm still wondering, actually. In my mind, I have become *that person.*

I'm not even sure what *that person* looks like. I am sure it's not quite good and not quite bad either, kind of like the peculiar older aunt every family has. The one that arrives with tales of adventures and cool gifts but stays a little too long with perfume that's a little too strong and stories that are a little more fish tale than an actual adventure.

I'm sure there is a stereotype of sorts here, but I can't put my finger on it. Am I that person who says goofy things and is not taken seriously? Or am I that person who says goofy things, is not taken seriously, and can get away with all kinds of stuff? Maybe I'm a dingbat like Edith on *All In The Family*. She was called a dingbat by her husband, but in reality, she was pretty deep. She was as spiritually connected as she could be in the seventies, as a wife to a racist, sexist, everything-phobic husband, but she was in stealth mode because it was safer.

Maybe being that person isn't all bad. I'm sure I am many things to different coworkers, and with the number of people I work with, it's probably best not to try and figure it all out anyway. I do like stealth spiritual mode, though. I'll try that on for a while.

SMITH AND JONES (NOT WESSON)

Do you know about the Beverly Hillbillies; the ones who moved from their one-room cabin in the hills of Kentucky to a mansion in Beverly Hills? Now, I doubt most of us are going to get a rifle and start shooting for our proverbial oil rush. But what if. . .? What if there is some metaphorical truth in there? I heard several things this week that still have the peanut gallery that is my brain buzzing and asking, *How do I know?* By now, I have come to learn and realize this particular query is a harbinger of sorts that a new door is opening. I had two conversations with two different women that made me curious. I will call the first woman Smith and the second, Jones.

Smith thought she was destined to be a high-powered, penthouse, Forbes 500, executive. Academically, she was well on her way with stellar grades and a top-notch internship that made most Ivy League business school grads drool with an imagined but rich, savory taste of the future. It is much like the kind of tantalizing "wish that was me" feeling you get when seeing a burger commercial before lunch, and you still have an hour to go! It was the kind of internship that gets you in the door and is very often not just the gateway, but the rolled-out red carpet to a phenomenal career. During her senior year, Smith was hand-picked by the board of directors for the company in which she was interning and handed over by her professors like a proud father giving away his daughter to be married. She was on her way!

Then she met a guy.

Not any guy. She met *the* guy. The one that got down on bended knee and asked her to be his missus. Smith said yes, and the babies started coming. After the first, she thought she'd resume the path of her career. She got pregnant again, and when number two was born, she again thought she'd resume her career path after he was a little bit older. She went through this one more time before succumbing to being a full-time mom of three. She raised a wonderful family and never looked back except, from time to time, to wonder, *How do I know . . . ?*

She raised her family over the years, and somewhere in there, she took to making homemade jams. They were *so* good that her family started requesting them. Then her friends did. She got so busy she actually opened her own business selling homemade jams and canned products. Twenty years after graduating, she put her degree and experience to use after all! She followed her heart in a way and manner she could have never imagined back when she was barely a glimmer in her professors' eyes.

I had a very different conversation with Jones. It was more of a monologue to which I was held captive. Jones got pregnant and she also started having kids. She was angry with her husband and children for the life she never had. She recounted events and memories to justify her blame and anger, all the while pointing the finger at them and violently poking the air for added, angry effect. She never let them be the life she was supposed to have.

To her, her life became a one-way super highway without a single exit. She just hurtled down the road, blindly speeding into a meaningless future for her lack of attention. Jones was so busy being angry about what could have been and so fixated on looking back at everything she had that was nothing she wanted, there was no possibility of seeing anything ahead of her. Because she was so intent on looking back, she occasionally smacked into opportunities in front of her. As the opportunity crashed and burned in front of Jones, she had limited insight into what was happening. The opportunity smoldered, and in the rising and fading smoke circles, she found something familiar and yet intangible, something like a waft of cologne that catches you unawares and reminds you of an ex . . . what was their name?

How do we know? How do we know what our divine path is and if we are on it or butting heads with it? What if it is just trial and error and the best fit wins? And how the hell do you know, do I know, if being a spiritual warrior for humanity looks like making and selling homemade jams? How do I know I'm not selling out for a paycheck as an occupational therapist instead of diving in feet first to follow an art career? And maybe the divine path is the one we are on anyway, and the one we are willing to walk. I have heard it said, "It is what we make it," and "It is because you say so." Perhaps. It also seems like more than that. Like if I really am on the path of my life's purpose, there is a certain grace and ease with which things happen and get done, not just because, "I say so." That grace and ease feels somewhat inherent. I'm not talking about ease like "piece of cake" ease, or "I got away with something" ease, but easy as in natural. "Easy like Sunday morning" ease. Regardless of the bumps, bruises, hiccups, stumbles, and trip-ups along the way, it is still easy.

Being an occupational therapist is like that for me. I struggled at Texas A&M. I struggled to get to class, study, and get the grades I needed and so, dropped out. One year later I transferred to Texas Women's University, and it was a different experience. Getting up, studying, and getting the necessary grades was much easier. My life flowed much better. So much so that my advisor, looking at my grades and transcript from A&M, flat-out asked me how I got into their OT program. I told her I just walked in. And it really was, literally and metaphorically, like just walking in. The next five years of school were also like that. I easily met each successive metric that moved me to the next level in the program, and it always felt as easy as "just walking in."

Now I am wondering what's next. I don't have kids or a family. They would be my next, my legacy. They would be the gift I give this world. But this is a developmental track laid down by the elders of psychology. I want to play a bigger game such that my *next* is not limited by, held to, or even within the parameters of developmental appropriateness. I want the next half of my life to be for something more than just paying the bills. I want the ladder I climb to get me much higher than the penthouse office or glass ceiling. So that brings me right back to the beginning. *How do I know?*

SOUTHERN SUMMERS

Southern summers caress a soul and tickle the senses
with warm winds, lazy afternoons and tender breezes.
Days are filled with the hum of life and a cicada song,
The evenings tender, golden, and long,
Joyous voices drift away
on the gentle winds of Sunday
through open windows wide
and past fluttering curtains aside
On the warm winds, children's play and laughter drifts
catching bubbles, raindrops, and cotton candy whiffs.
In the night, lightning bugs set the sky aglow
and heat loosens its palorous grip to let the day go
But still the laughter rises and giggles ripple.
Play is familiar, timeless, and simple;
long into the night until the hour looms bigger,
one by one familiar lights flicker

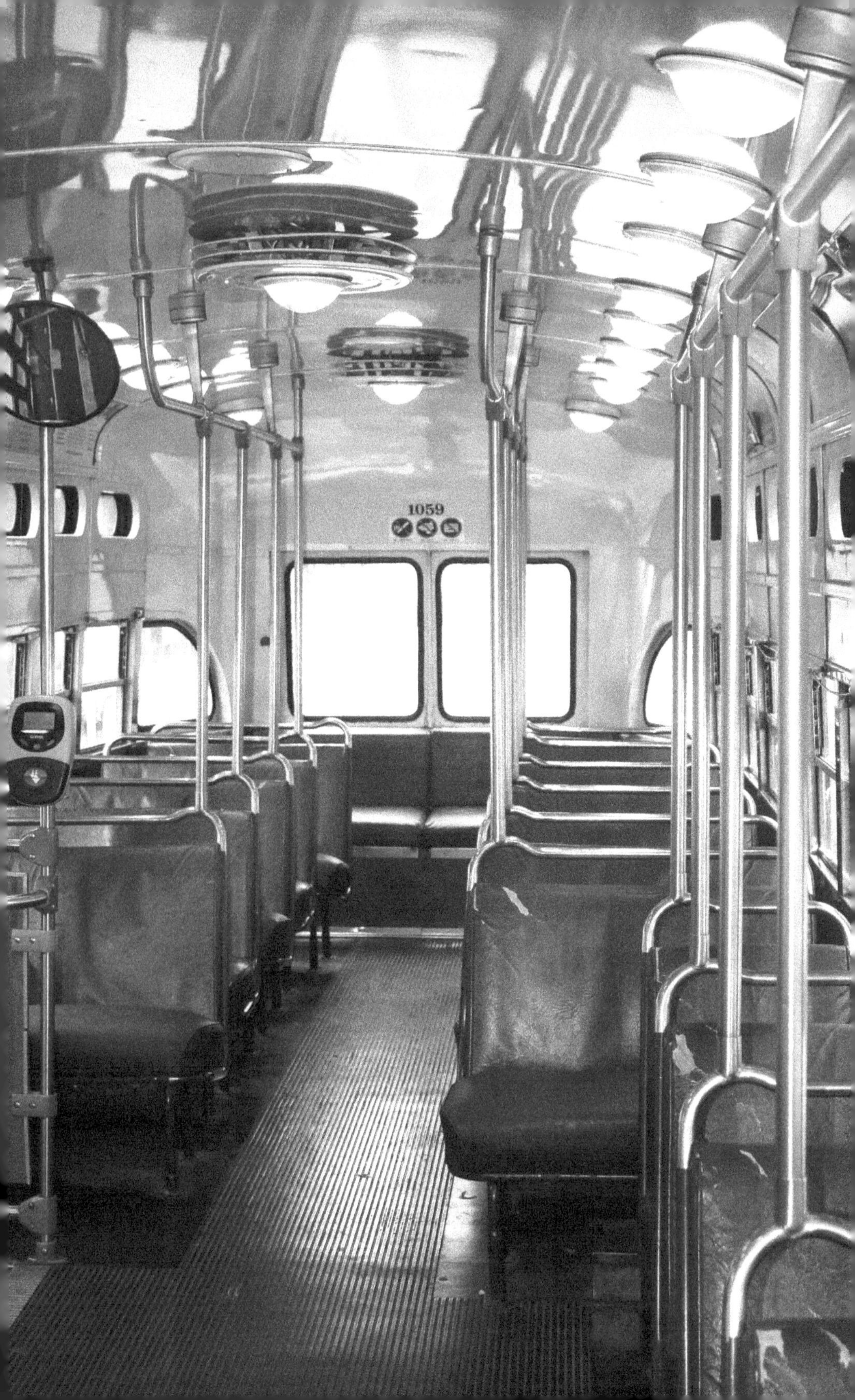
1059

OFFENDED

I was sitting at my kitchen table, sipping my morning coffee and trying to wake up, when I stumbled upon an article listing things not to say if you want to sound classy. As I scanned the list, I couldn't help but chuckle. Many of the items have long since blurred and bled into common culture, and I'm not sure anyone would even notice their absence, let alone associate it with being classy. I mean, not swearing, or ending a sentence with a preposition? Come on, us regular bastards don't need an article to tell us where the juiciness is at.

While that was a feeble attempt at some form of humor, those who truly know me, know I CANNOT stand when well-meaning people end their sentences in a preposition. I'm covert about my grammar snobbery. If you've made it this far in the book, then you know I'm not opposed to the f-word and other colorful expletives that my Mormon editors routinely feel the need to manage. I can swear like a sailor, I know I can, and if my mom were still alive, she would have a thing or two—or twenty—to say about it.

Anyway…as I continued reading the article, I noticed that it wasn't just about grammar and profanity. Some of the phrases on the list were deemed inappropriate due to cultural appropriation, and that's a whole other can of worms.

Now, cultural appropriation can be a tricky thing to navigate,

"

especially in a country of immigrants like ours. I remember living in Pakistan as a kid and coming back to the States at seven years old, which, at that tender age, was just another move. In Milwaukee, I was making chapatis and wearing saris like it was normal. It didn't take me long to convert to wearing corduroy pants and sweaters. And here in Texas, we love our tacos, guacamole, chips, and salsa. Is that cultural appropriation? Some might say yes, but I say pass the hot sauce!

Anyway, I've decided life is too short to get offended by every little thing people might say to me. Sure, folks make mistakes or sometimes don't know any better. And let's face it, some people are just plain mean and aren't going to change their ways, no matter how much we get our feelings hurt. I'd rather save my energy and walk away from them than waste my breath trying to educate them on how to be nice to me.

I've been around long enough to see the terms "colored people" change to "black people" and then to "African-Americans," and "oriental people" become "Asian." I even had a guardian in high school who was half Puerto Rican and called herself an HBRK—a half-breed roach kicker. I'm still not exactly sure what that meant, but those of us who loved her called her that, too. If anyone dared say something even remotely close to that in any other context, she'd just walk away and not give it a second thought.

Ultimately, all these politically correct changes are getting too many to keep up with, and I know I'm bound to slip up and offend someone without meaning to. I think so much of our current obsession with political correctness is just a misguided attempt to mandate kindness. The idea seems to be that by eliminating certain words, phrases, or expressions, we're automatically being nice. But maybe if we were all just genuinely kind to one another, none of this would matter.

The thing is, it's hard to forgive the past when the future shows little promise of change. We can legislate political correctness until the cows come home, but we can't legislate kindness. And if that's what we're trying to do, well, I'd say we're falling short of the mark by a country mile. There are mean people everywhere and given their dispositions, I'm guessing they have no intention of listening to my monologue on being kind, much less changing.

So, if you'll excuse me, I'm going to finish my coffee, maybe make a few chapatis, and try to spread a little kindness in this world. And if I happen to end a sentence with a preposition, or accidentally offend someone along the way, well, I'll just have to hope they'll find it in their hearts to forgive me. After all, we're all muddling through this life together, one faux pas at a time.

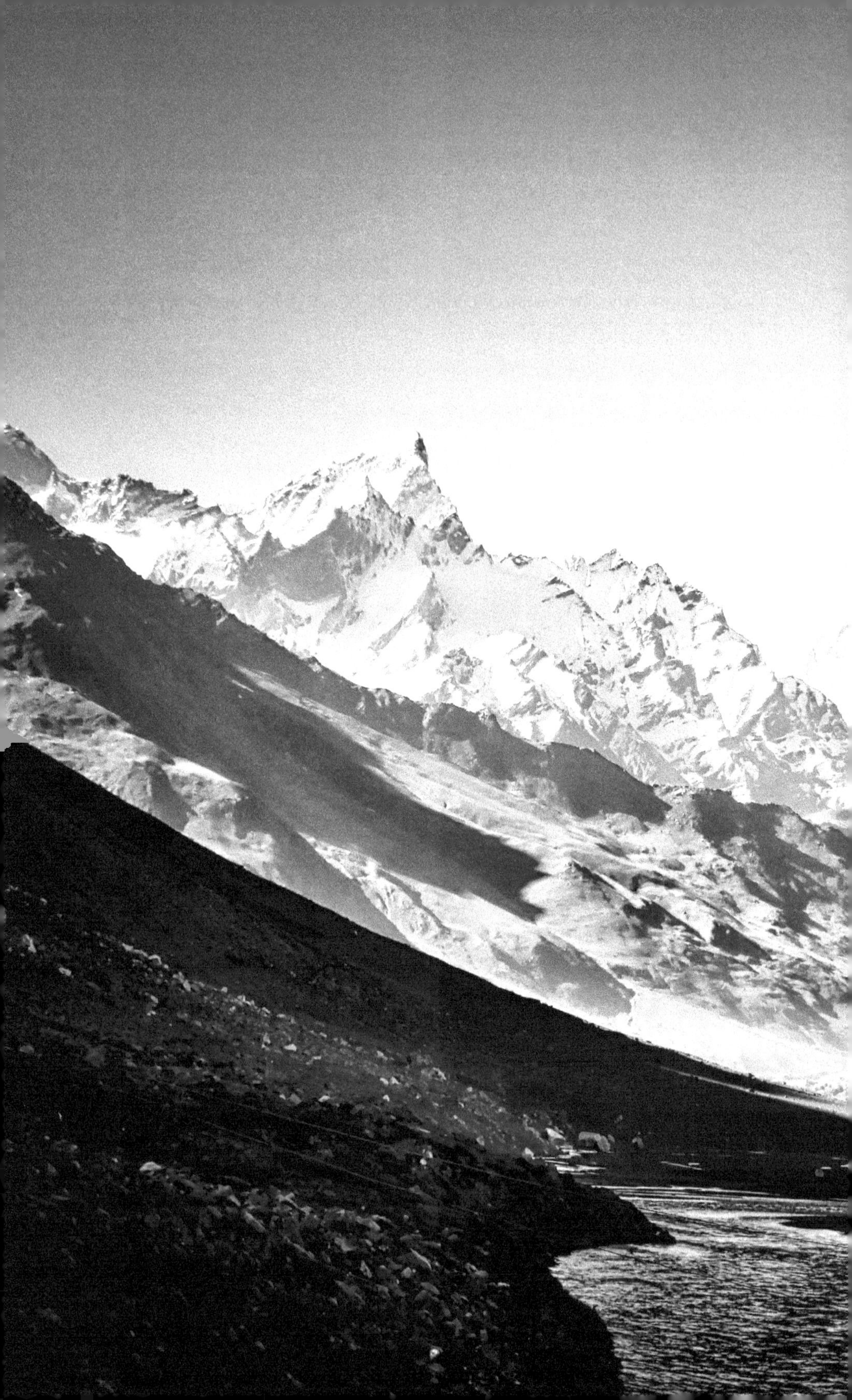

PLEASE FORGIVE ME

I was listening to a podcast that strayed a bit from its initial topic and started to talk about "The pinnacle of forgiveness is to forget." This got me thinking, because my knee-jerk reaction was, "Like hell!" From there I began to review many of the transgressions against me and wondered if I could "forget." So my opinion is this: forgiveness is a human endeavor. Forgetting comes from the divine in all of us. It's not like erasing our memories or history, but rather the ability to stop punishing people for the rest of their lives. One of the many ironies of life is that when I punish someone for all eternity, I am the one that is really stuck. They, in all likelihood, have moved on.

I wondered if I could forgive my dad for permanently altering and scarring the landscape of our family with his cheating. Can I forgive him for driving my mom to a suicide attempt? Can I forgive my mom for drinking too much and making me a teenage surrogate parent to my younger sister? Can I forgive the boys that bullied me in school? Can I forgive the ex who cheated on me and who stole thousands of dollars while I turned my attention from her to the care of my dying mother? Can I forgive another ex, the one who slowly, stealthily isolated me from my friends and family so no one, could point out what an unhealthy relationship it was?

Yes. I can.

Can I forget these events? Forget them as an act of injustice, wrongness, brutality, stupidity, or not knowing differently? Can I forget such that I can have a loving conversation with my dad instead of talks rife with digs and silent *f-yous*? Can I forget so that I remember my exes as the day we met instead of as the reasons we parted? Can I forget so that what I do and create next does not come from a foundation of bitterness or hate?

Sometimes, I think, being a victim gives me permission to maintain the status quo. I'm not saying roll over and pretend like nothing happened, like it's okay. It's not okay. None of it is okay. But in the wake of those events and more, I'm the one stuck in the turbulence of those murky waters. Everyone that was a part of those events of my life has likely moved on. Most never looked back. It was just me, in my hurt, in my wailing of how unfair life is, in my cries of how people suck. I got stuck there in that raw, emotional place where nothing heals. All new transgressions piled on top of the old ones, as I collected one traumatic event after another.

Victim that I can be, I know I have dished out my own variety of sordid, dirty, reprehensible behaviors as well.

Can I forgive myself? Uuummmm, maybe.

Can I forgive? Yes.

Can I forget? . . . Yes

Am I skittish? Yes!

But this is me. And then there is us. You and me. And I don't know how or where to begin. I don't know how to ask if you can forgive, if you can forget, if you can move on. I don't know how to ask so that we can alter the foundation upon which the future is being built, so that our ancestors can rest knowing our legacy is much bigger than theirs. For all the *isms*: sexism, racism, ageism; for all the phobias: homophobia, xenophobia; for all the alls that divide us, hurt us, it takes someone willing to not retaliate. It takes someone willing to be the one who walks away because he or she is not willing to fight anymore. It takes someone willing to start stopping. I'm not sure I know how to do this, and I sure don't know how to ask you to.

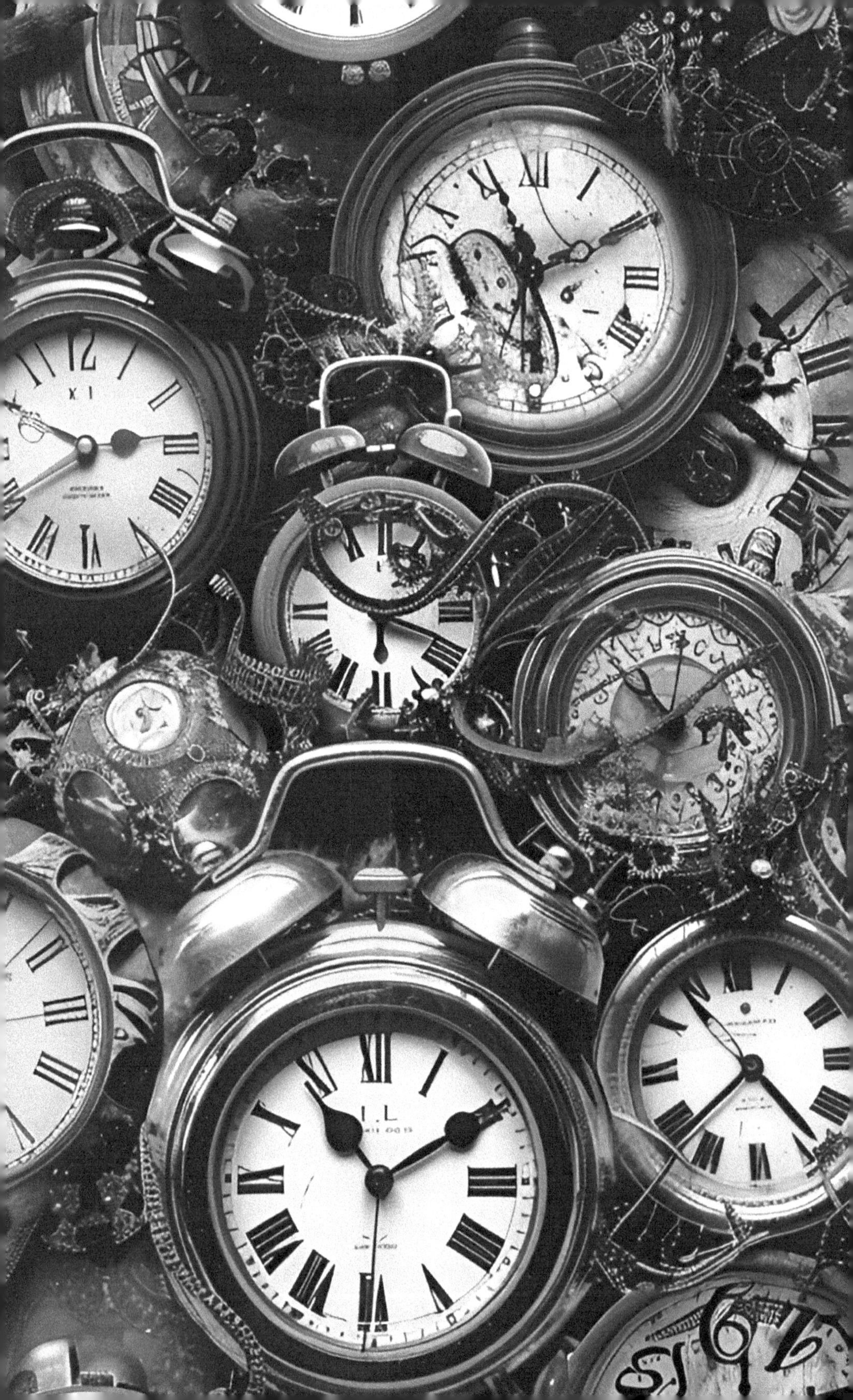

FOUR MINUTES

I always enjoy the walk in to work from the outpost we call a parking lot, even if it becomes a jog because of escaping time and the call of the clock. The seconds tick menacingly in my brain like the alarm-clock-swallowing crocodile that stalks Captain Hook in *Peter Pan*. This walk, though sometimes brief, gives me the chance to enjoy a beautiful day before holing up for ten hours. Today happens to be appreciable with a soul-satisfying sunrise announcing the day. I briefly go down the rabbit hole that today is not given, it is a gift . . . but I am yanked out of that particular thread of gratitude by the deafening sound of the time passing.

Tick. Tick. Tick.

Despite the beauty of this morning, I am all in my head, strategizing my arrival time and jockeying for a position within the mass of coworkers, all posturing to get the best spot possible. All the while, the night shift hasn't quite left, and the morning shift is just arriving, making available parking as sparse as rain in summer. This morning was no exception.

Tick. Tick. Tick.

Finally, out of my car and making my way to the front door, I grit my teeth and chance a glance at my watch. I have four minutes on the plus side. That is time enough to get in, get an elevator to my floor, and punch the clock.

What's funny is how this same four minutes is plenty of time today, but when I was rushing to a meeting yesterday, it was not enough time at all. How can the same time be so different in different situations, to a multitude of people, and in a variety of circumstances?

When I was a kid, it felt like it took ten years just to get to summer break. Waiting through the month of May for the summer bell to ring took nine of those years. And then, finally in the throes of summer break, it was just mere minutes until the school bell rang an the beginning of the new school year.

There are many days at work I am rushing to beat the clock and get out before it flips into overtime. One very odd day, I was done fifteen minutes early. That was the slowest fifteen minutes I have experienced to date, waiting for the clock to chime "time to go." How does this happen? How do I experience 6:22 so differently from my neighbor, my sister, or anybody else?

On a bit of a same but different note, my sister and I are less than one year apart in age. To be exact, we are fifty-one weeks apart. We grew up in the same house, with the same parents, and went to the same school with the exception of once—my first year of high school was her last of junior high school. We get together now and tell tales of our childhood, and it amazes me how different our recollections are.

Four minutes are four minutes are four minutes. They don't get repackaged or rebranded or get a do-over. They are the same two hundred and forty seconds. Every. Single. Time.

Then why do they never seem the same?

There are natural cycles in the universe: the rotation of the earth, the cycle of the seasons, and the coming and going of night and day, but time as we know it is a man-made construct. And if time is a man-made construct, it seems like a design flaw to me.

CHURCH

I went to church today; it wasn't in a steepled building with stained-glass windows. It was in a parking lot, where I listened to a homeless man express gratitude for the many blessings he felt he had. Everything he owned was lumped together in and around a dirty duffle bag. I doubt all his possessions would exceed the number of fingers and toes I have. Speaking with him, I felt exponentially more grateful for what I had, and a little guilty for missing the things I did not have, but felt I needed. The reality is, I have more than I need, and, in all honesty, I have more than I want.

I went to church today but not to a place dotted with identical pews and a brass-piped organ. It was the hospital where I work. I listened to a young mother recount her car accident. She was probably an immigrant, probably illegal, spoke very little English, and did not have much in the way of material possessions. She was t-boned by an underaged drunk driver, who totaled her only means of transportation. The accident paralyzed her, killed her elementary school-aged nephew, and severely injured another child. The remaining five kids in her late-model minivan were okay—physically, anyway. She refused to press charges, and instead, forgave the thirteen-year-old drunk driver, stating, "So many lives are already ruined. Why ruin another?"

I went to church today, and the people streaming in and out

were not dressed in their Sunday best; they wore uniforms and work boots. Today it was at 7-Eleven. The cashier, probably not making much more than minimum wage, bought a homeless man hot coffee on a cold day. Normally, the 7-Eleven staff run homeless people off because the homeless run the customers off. But today, she broke from what should be done, and did what needed to be done.

BULLY

The dictionary definition of bully:

noun, plural bul·lies

A blustering, mean, or predatory person who intimidates, abuses, harasses, or coerces people, especially those considered unlikely to defend themselves: *playground bullies targeting younger children or children with disabilities; a workplace bully who cuts me off when I speak*

verb (used with object), bul·lied, bul·ly·ing.

To act the bully toward; habitually intimidate, abuse, or harass: *The boy next door constantly bullies the younger children in the neighborhood.*

To coerce or compel by bullying: *The salesman bullied me into upgrading the car's paint protection and rust-proofing.*

One of several obsolete definitions of bully is *sweetheart, darling.* For me, there is an irony about this now long-forgotten definition.

Like so many kids, then and now, I was bullied. It was my last year of junior high; my ninth-grade year, and it may have gone on longer had we not moved out of state at the end of the school year. When I first went to my parents about the way I was being treated, they explained I was getting this unwanted attention because the boy who was bullying me liked me, and because we were thirteen, he didn't know how to express himself.

John was tall for his age, standing two heads above most of us kids. He was even taller than most teachers. His hair was a disorganized mass, thick, tightly curled, and espresso brown, making him seem even taller. He was a six-foot chunk of nastiness, gangly and freckled, and he wore heavy-framed glasses that he constantly pushed up his nose. Don't feel sorry for him, though. He was also mean and emotionally damaging, the details of which are more suited for a conversation over a beer or two.

These days, I feel like there is some desensitization around bullies and bullying. Personally, I take issue with the last part of this definition: "a workplace bully who cuts me off when I speak." After enduring the bullying heaped on me as a kid, being interrupted when I speak, as an adult, seems better categorized as bad manners.

I grew up as the Information Age also grew. I remember a world in which we were not so individually and collectively tethered to one another. We did not have a twenty-four/seven news cycle, or twenty-four/seven anything, for that matter. Our phones were at home, not in our pockets, with a *very* long cord that reached into the linen closet or bathroom for privacy. With the creation of social media, I can connect/reconnect with people from my childhood who, when I moved half the country away, would have otherwise become distant memories instead of in-my-face realities. I am so very happy for the few high school friends who sought me out because I thought they were lost forever.

Though I had no desire to reconnect with John, the boy who bullied me, I looked for him on Facebook from time to time. I can't tell you why I did this, because it ripped off the scab that formed over that particular wound. Every. Single. Time. I imagine it's like the compulsion to stare at the mangled destruction of life and property when passing a horrific car accident.

For many years, I never found him, but a few months ago, I did. I looked at the pictures, and I saw a guy smiling, hanging out with friends and family; a very normal guy, perhaps a blue-collar, hardworking guy. A guy who looked like he had a daughter or granddaughter. And he looked happy, and I was happy for him. I did not see that coming! While I will never know the truth behind those pictures, they altered the words of at least one of my childhood stories.

Something shifted for me. Not on purpose. Not because I spent years in therapy or reading self-help books, but it shifted nonetheless. Divine intervention did for me what I was unable to do for myself. I can move on, because clearly, he did. His hurtful words began to rearrange themselves into a different narrative. While the faint images of those erased words are still there, they are indeed faint, much like a wound that has healed leaving behind only a scar. And a scar, too, continues to fade with time.

And now, forty years later, it's okay; I am okay.

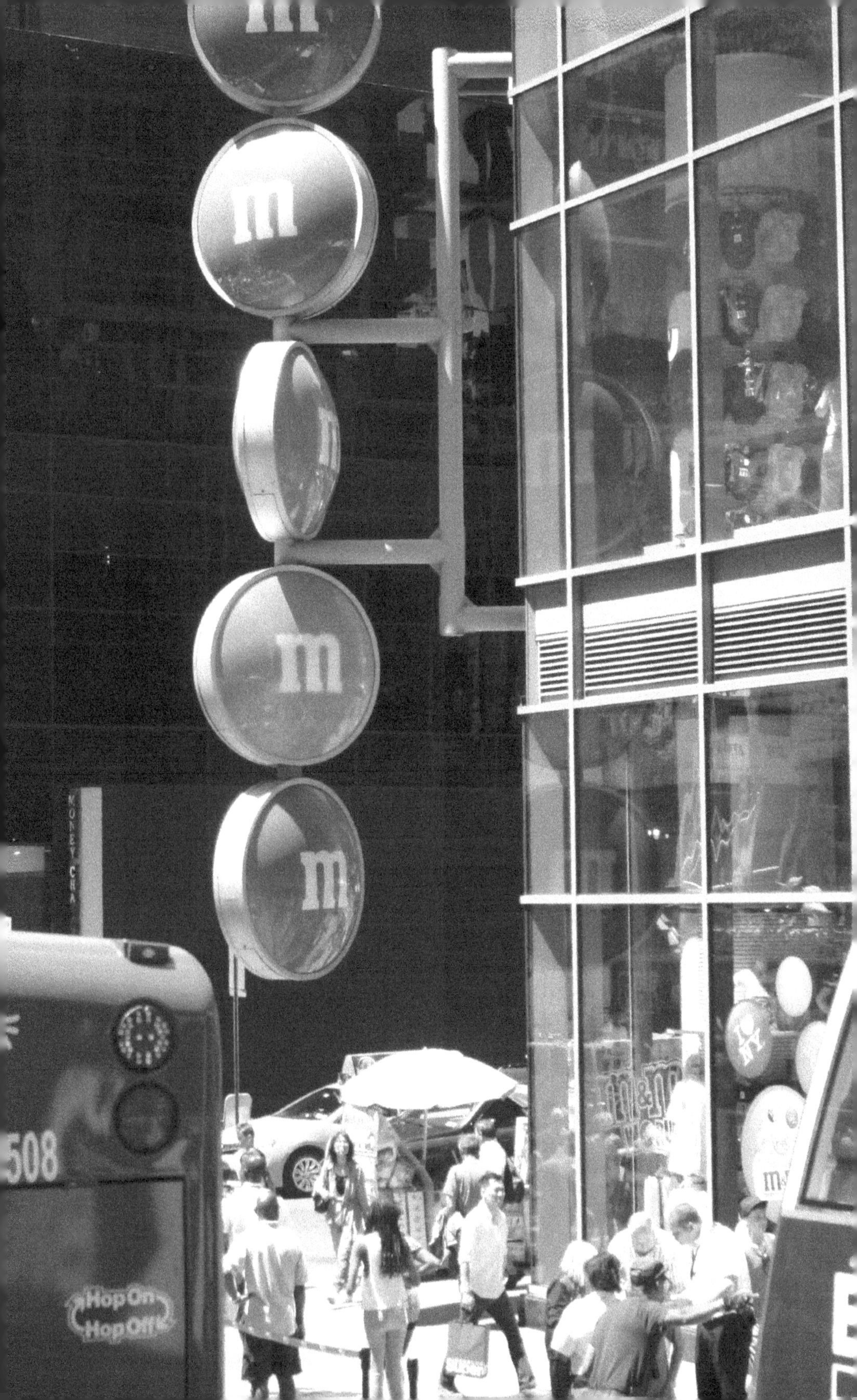

m
m
m
m
508
Hop On
Hop Off

OKAY BOOMER

More and more there are things that remind me I am getting older. My body, for one, is a constant source of those reminders. The barrage of aches and pains, the stiffness, and the alarming rate at which I have started moving slowly are just a few examples. Every time I get a new ache, I do a brief check of my family history and run through a mental list. Should I go to the doctor? Was it there yesterday? What could I have done to cause it? Sadly, the answer is nothing. I don't have to do anything to hurt. No weekend warrior shenanigans, no bragging about what I did at the gym, or anything else. All I have to do is get out of bed.

I knew I had crossed a line when, early on in my time working at the hospital, I came home to tell Kris about my day and referred to my coworkers as "those kids I work with." Ten years later we have a new batch of "kids" coming through. They are our students, some with a deer-in-the-headlights look on their young faces, some a bit overconfident, and some constantly lost in the maze we call work.

I am fifty-five and proudly, defiantly, GenX. We didn't wear helmets or knee pads when we skateboarded or rode our bikes, and when we banged ourselves up, no one was at home to put us back together because both parents were usually working. We drank from water hoses, left the house at sunup Saturday morning to run with friends, and returned in time for dinner. Our parents never worried about us like they do today when kids are gone all day.

We didn't have cell phones, and we certainly couldn't be tracked by some dot on a screen. We got the phone with the longest cord in the house and went into the bathroom or a closet for privacy to talk with our BFF. In our house, we had two phones. One upstairs and one downstairs. If you were stealth enough, you could quietly pick up the other phone and listen in.

During my GenX childhood, the TV started airing at five in the morning. PBS was the first station to come on, and it aired *Hatha Yoga*. It went off the air at midnight, playing "The National Anthem." After that, it was nothing but silence and the color bars on the screen. There was no CNN or MTV. And when there was MTV, it really was just music videos— no *Teen Mom*, *Big Brother*, or *Buckwild*. I watched the emergence of wireless phones and cable TV, the disappearance of the newspaper, the rise of social media and online dating, and the fall of privacy.

As I grew up, I heard older people complain about my generation and how we were lazy, self-centered, good-for-nothing kids. They were afraid to put their future into our delinquent hands.

Now old enough to have watched two generations grow up, Millennials and GenZ, I am not as afraid for my future as were my parents and grandparents afraid for theirs. If the past dictates the future at all, I am confident the Millennials and GenZ kids will continue to evolve and outgrow some of their youth and stereotypical assignments. That being said, I don't think there has been a generation about which more complaints have been lodged than the Millennials. They in turn volley back at the Baby Boomers their version of a battle cry, "Okay, Boomer!" Some Boomers may not know how to set up their cell phone, but some GenZ kids do not know how to do simple repairs or live life without a credit card or cell phone or social media.

Today I said goodbye to one of our students. He was neither a deer in headlights nor overconfident. He was eager to learn and didn't shrink from our constructive criticism. As a young person, he was able to allay any concerns about my future, and his future certainly is bright as it opens up before him one step at a time. In this moment, there is no responsibility for him to shoulder, that comes later.

The kids I work with work hard. They also play hard. They've started getting married and having kids of their own, and while I worry about what Social Security funds will be left for me and my golden years, they take care of themselves and live like tomorrow is not promised. I think there may not be any Social Security left for me when I retire, but they go on like Social Security will be a long-forgotten fairytale.

We have gone from one phone in every home to a phone in every pocket that is exponentially faster and more powerful than the mainframe computers of the eighties. We also have driverless vehicles, AI, identity theft, and video cameras EVERYWHERE. Looking back, it seems like there has been more change in the last twenty-five years of my life than the first twenty-five. It leaves me emphatically curious about the next twenty-five and the next generation. What will we call them, and what will we complain about? And by that time, the Millennials and GenZ kids will be complaining about them too. It's just the way it goes.

"What is happening to our young people? They disrespect their elders, they disobey their parents. They ignore the law. They riot in the streets, inflamed with wild notions," said Plato, in the fourth century BC. In a world where things are changing faster than I can keep up with, or care to, there are those things that *never* change.

THE SUN COMES UP

The sun came up again
with little comfort,
for the morning wane
As we take an agonal breath
and struggle to find decency,
in what remains before death
Helping ourselves first,
hurtling along like a runaway train,
we try to quench an insatiable thirst
We ride rusty old rails
with the most precious cargo;
into the long black night on abandoned trails.
While quietly waits Providence
and begs no one to its door
but invites with graciousness.
All can come to the table
with a lowered head and lifted heart
to receive the truth and bury the fable

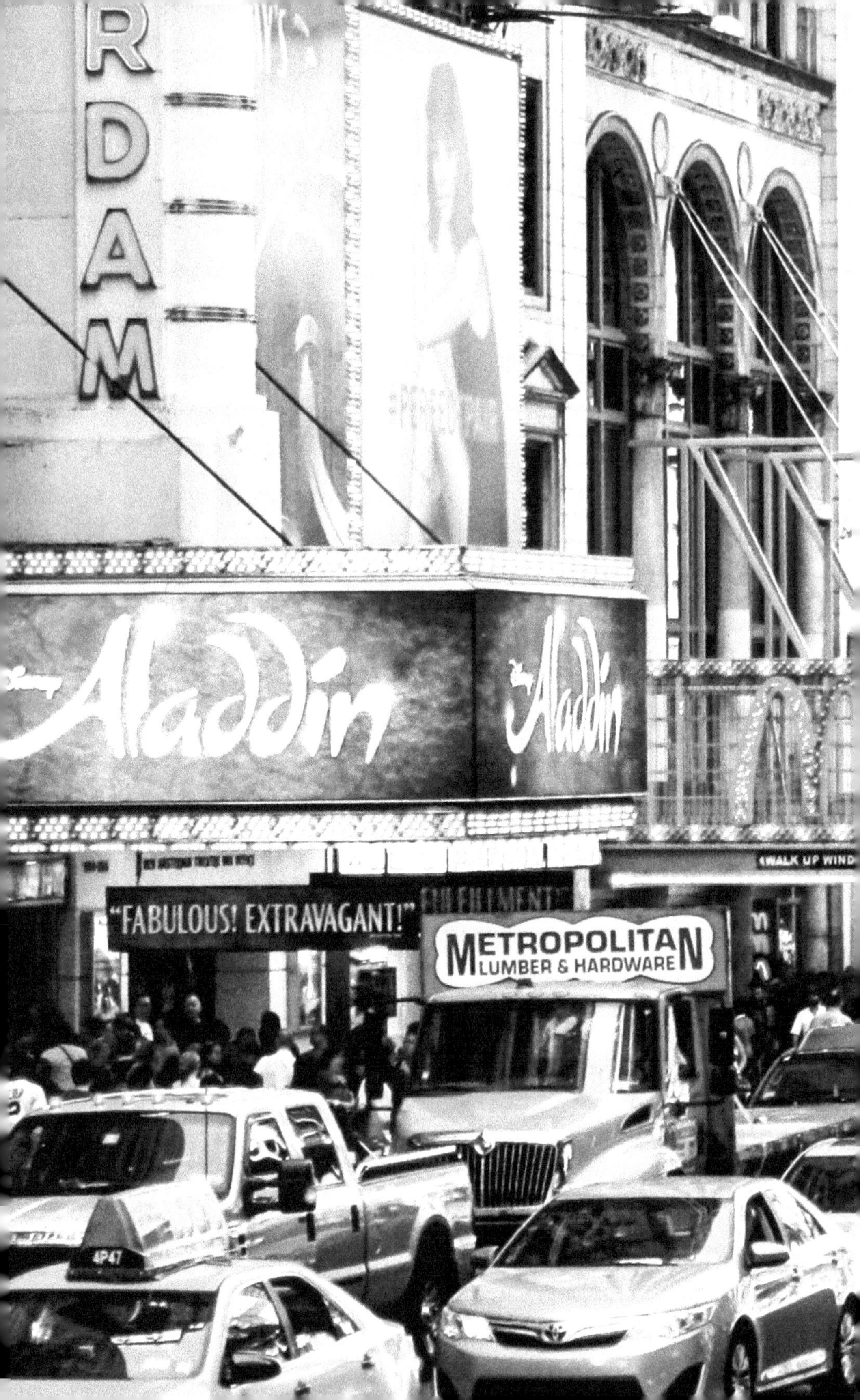
RDAM
Disney Aladdin
Disney Aladdin
"FABULOUS! EXTRAVAGANT!"
METROPOLITAN
LUMBER & HARDWARE
WALK UP WIND

TURN LEFT

Have you seen the movie *The Second Best Exotic Marigold Hotel*? It's a sneaky one for sure. It started out slowly and made me wonder why I kept watching. But there was an undercurrent that got me and swept me up until I was completely lost in the movie.

It is about a group of seniors—as in age, not school—from London, who are dissatisfied with their retirement options and set out to find what else is available to them. Their inquiry takes them to India and the Second Best Exotic Marigold Hotel.

By the end of the movie, some of them stay and some decide to go back home. One of the characters, while stuck in traffic in a rickshaw and waiting to make a right turn toward the airport for her flight back to London, announces to her husband that she is actually going to stay. Throughout the movie, this couple is subtly (they are English, after all) quite unhappy with each other, their lives together, and their lives individually.

He asks with an air of disbelief and confusion, "What are you doing?"

For the first time in the movie, she smiles and tells him she loves him, then replies, "I am turning left."

She had followed the seemingly calm current of her life and the path of least resistance. She did all that was expected of her. Everything was good, until it wasn't. In her later years, she makes a bold choice to be happy. She tells her husband she is turning left, and in doing so creates a profound and far-reaching ripple effect, much like the Butterfly Effect in chaos theory.

Sometimes not all tidal waves are bad. What was good for her was good for those around her as well, though it did not seem like it at first.

Spoiler alert: her husband ended up happier also.

YOU ARE OKAY

You just fell.
Maybe it's the pain
of a scraped knee,
a shattered bone,
or a broken heart.
But you are okay.
Get back up.
It will hurt a bit,
maybe a lot.
So you'll limp for a while,
but you're standing
and you are okay.
Put one foot in front.
And now the other.
You'll wobble a bit;
you may stumble.

But you are walking.
And you are okay.
Look straight ahead.
See where you are going.
Now look back.
You may not want to,
afraid to start over;
but you are moving
and you are okay.
See the corner
and get ready to turn.
Walk a little faster,
maybe even run.
You're living again.
You really are okay.

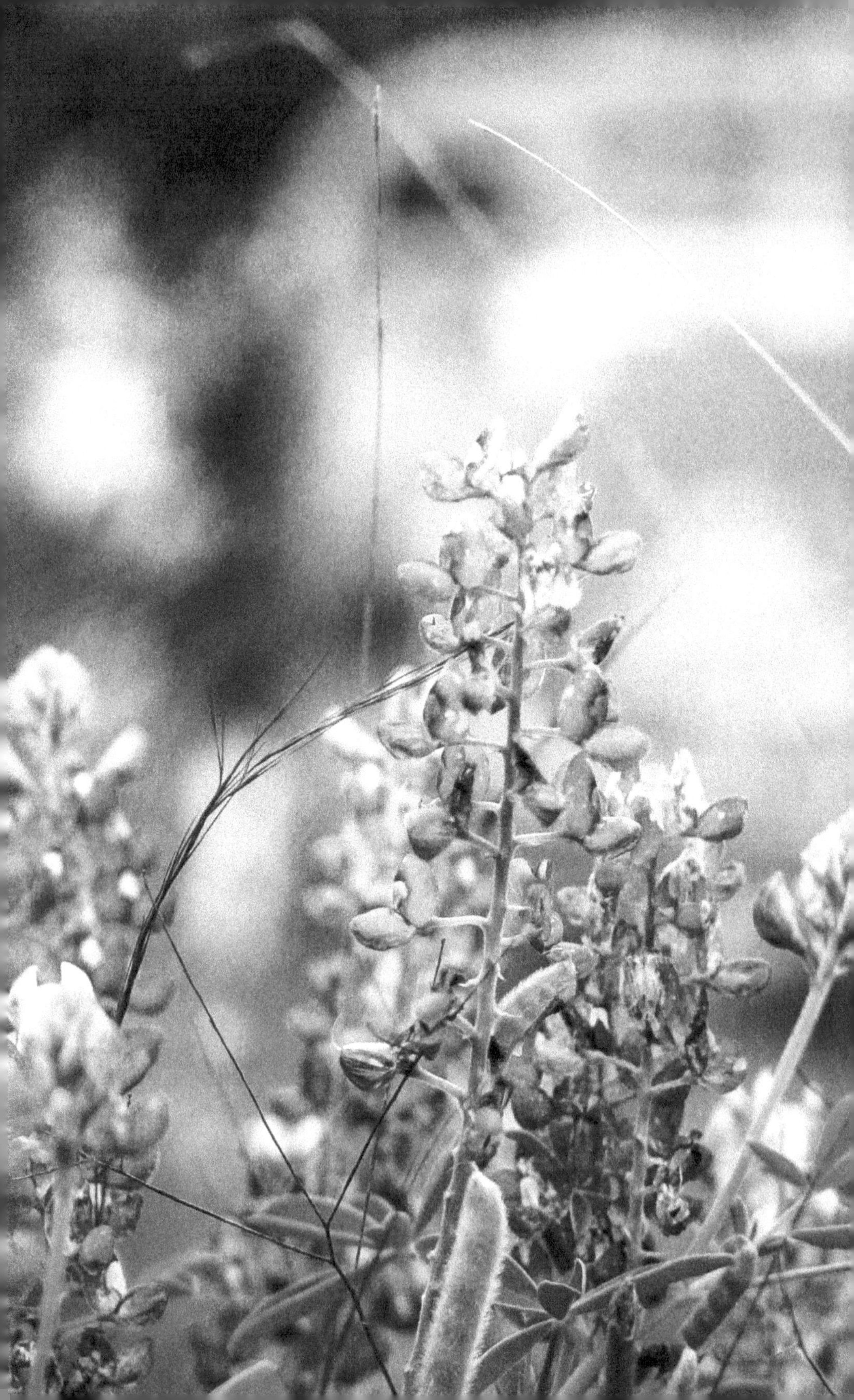

MEANWHILE, IN THE REST OF THE WORLD

I am a Texan. While I was born to parents who were on-the-run corporate nomads, I have now been in Texas longer than anywhere else. This is both currently and collectively true because I have tried to leave a couple of times but keep coming back.

We are the Lone Star State, and there is a "hold my beer" mentality among us. "Hold my beer, I got this," as in, "I don't need help." "Hold my beer, I'll do it," as in, "The whole lot of you couldn't do it but I can." There is no "we" in Texas unless it is the family unit. Then really, it is just a bigger "I." We are known to take care of our own; again, a bigger version of "I."

We were even once our own country called the Republic of Texas until 1845, when we agreed to join the Union. Talks of succession still rise up today. Texans are a pioneering, entrepreneurial, creative bunch that, due to the vastness of space, learned really fast "the cavalry ain't coming." We had to get the job done on our own. Even now, as many farms and ranch estates have been replaced by urban neighborhoods, the Lone Star mentality is still strong.

This week, the idea of getting things done on our own bit us in our collective ass. This week, Texas froze. Roads iced over, pipes broke all over town, power went out, and water was shut off. And a place that is usually "hotter 'n hell" came to an icy halt, sliding into *The Guinness Book of World Records*. Our power grid is independent of a shared network of neighboring states. And this week, Texans not so covertly became "we." We took care of each other; we helped our neighbors, and we opened our hearts to strangers as total chaos engulfed us. This week we staggered out of our oneness and helped each other. Jeep owners drove healthcare workers to their jobs and home again. Those who could venture out brought groceries for those who couldn't. Those who had heat opened up homes and businesses for those who didn't.

As people with a heart and an ever-expanding view of "we," we can send love, intention, and prayers. Send whatever is generated from your particular belief system. For my purposes, I say love and energy. We can send love and energy to Africa for a peaceful resolution for the best and highest good of all. We can send love and energy for the safety and well-being of our fellow humans in India and Japan. We can send love and energy for equality, to end hunger, for safe drinking water, and to those who are boots on the ground.

The time will come when we are called to do more, but for now, this works. A study was done some years ago. A group of women in Korea wanted to get pregnant. The women were split into two groups. Group A was the focus of a prayer group; Group B was left to their own devices. Group A ended up with more pregnancies. I don't know additional details like control, variability, and other details significant to a study. The takeaway is prayers, love, energy . . . there is something to it. So send love, send energy, send prayers.

And meanwhile, in the rest of the world, a soldier put his gun down, a child is fed, girls and women feel safe, young boys are freed from being child soldiers. And maybe, just maybe, a baby can be born into the world who will know of our current nightmares only from tales and legends.

NOT ON PURPOSE

Sing me a song where the sun doesn't shine,
and the hero hurts sometimes;
fights to get back up and slips on a broken promise
of love and hope and lost renaissance
Paint me a picture of clouds and storms
and the victor is not but forlorn
Where lies in quiet desperation
The slave of forgotten emancipation

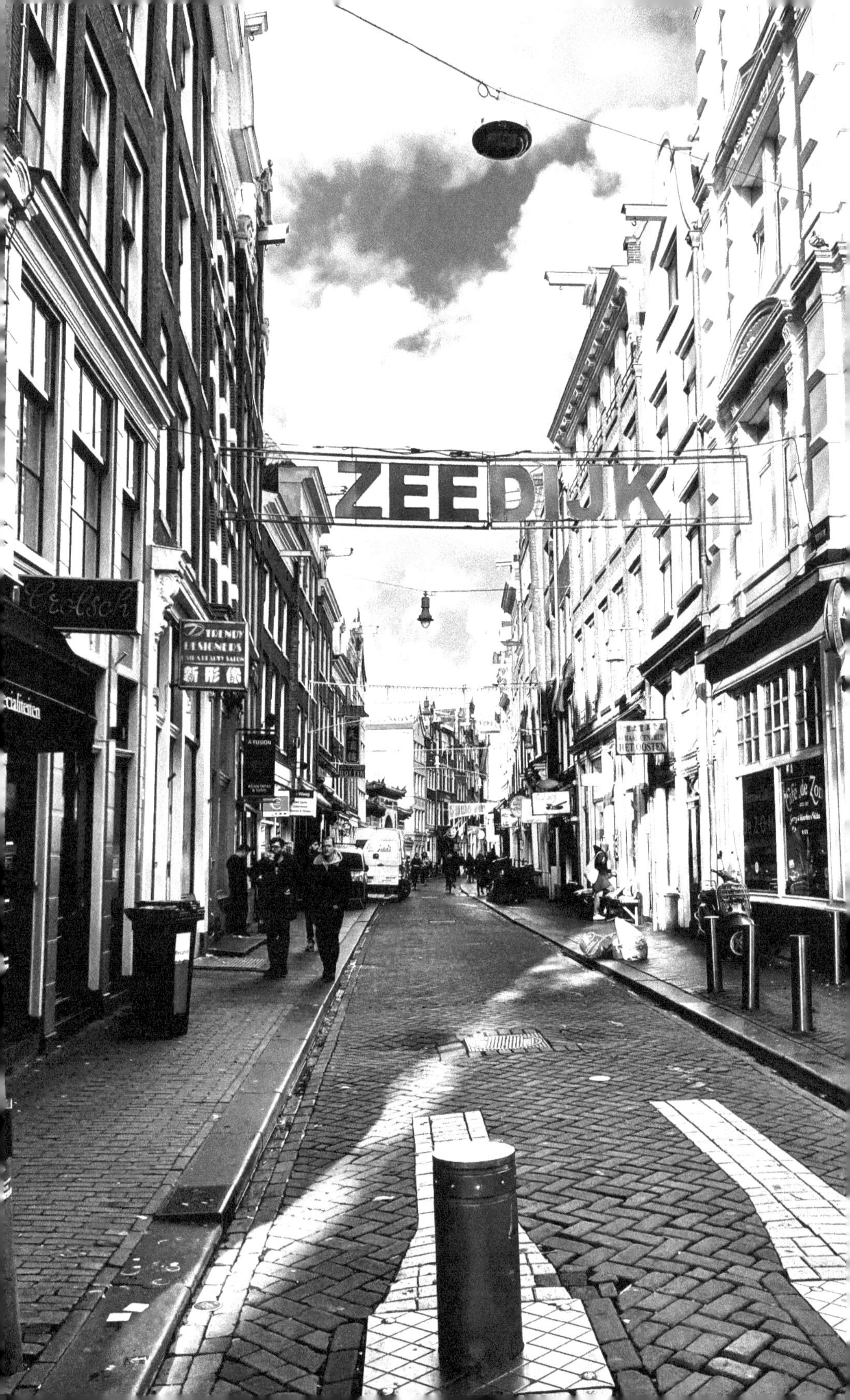

ZEEDIJK
TRENDY DESIGNERS
新形象

SAGE-ISH

I was asked once, "What sage advice would you give your fifteen-year-old self?"

All the typical answers flooded my brain like, "*Follow your dreams, even if they lead you to a career in underwater basket weaving; Listen to Grampa's stories, even if they're the same ones you've heard a million times (and pretend to be surprised by the plot twists); Don't let the mean girls get to you, and punch the bully harder (but aim for the solar plexus, it's more effective).*"

While these polite, proverbial platitudes had their place, they weren't the magic words I wished someone had told me. No, none of those really hit the mark.

What I really wanted to tell the younger me was to hang on, because being an adult can be fun (when you're not drowning in bills and responsibilities, that is). Woven intricately and in between the soul-crushing obligations of adulthood, are the less responsible things that give life a bit of color.

For instance, now, as an adult, I get to run outside in my socks all the time. I still hear Mom's voice yelling at me to put my shoes on so I don't ruin my socks (because apparently, socks are made of gold and unicorn hair), but I do it anyway. There's a guilty pleasure in it that leaves me feeling like I'm getting away with something (take that, Mom!).

Another perk to adulthood, my cars don't have to be practical, unlike the Mercury station wagon we had growing up, which was about as cool as a fanny pack and had the turning radius of a cruise ship.

My favorite vehicle was my Subaru WRX, a little sports car. It always threw off the valet guys when they saw this gray-haired woman get out of it (they probably thought I stole it from my nephew). I loved speeding up on the curves in that car, and the best ones are the Dallas North Tollway's Addison curves. The loose S-curve begged the Subaru for higher RPMs and lower gears!

But the best thing about being an adult, is that I don't have to stay in toxic situations—unless I'm related to them, then I'm stuck for life.

Once at work, I had been yelled at, cussed at, and called all kinds of names for the better part of the day. I walked into the room of my last patient, who immediately started yelling at me. I was three or four steps in, but as soon as I heard the first of that variety of colorful expletives, I turned around and walked right out the door I walked in. I didn't even stop. Thank God I'm an occupational therapist and not a nurse. They don't get that option.

But what I love to do most, and is perhaps a little controversial, is this little thing: (just-because-I-can-doesn't-mean-I-should-but-I-do) drop the *F-Bomb*.

Use it wisely.

Yes, as an adult, I'll swear like a sailor (a very angry, very drunk sailor), but it takes a lot for me to get to the point of telling someone to f*** off, and when I do, I won't get grounded or have to wash my mouth out with soap. Let's be honest, though, that never really worked with me anyway. Sometimes, I'd really get into it, and pretend like I was eating Old Spice ice cream!

In short, if I could've given my younger self some sage advice, it would've been this...Enjoy adulthood. Sure, it comes with some sucky things like responsibility, body deterioration, and taxes, but getting to do the little things you want is like a super-power, minus the spandex and cape.

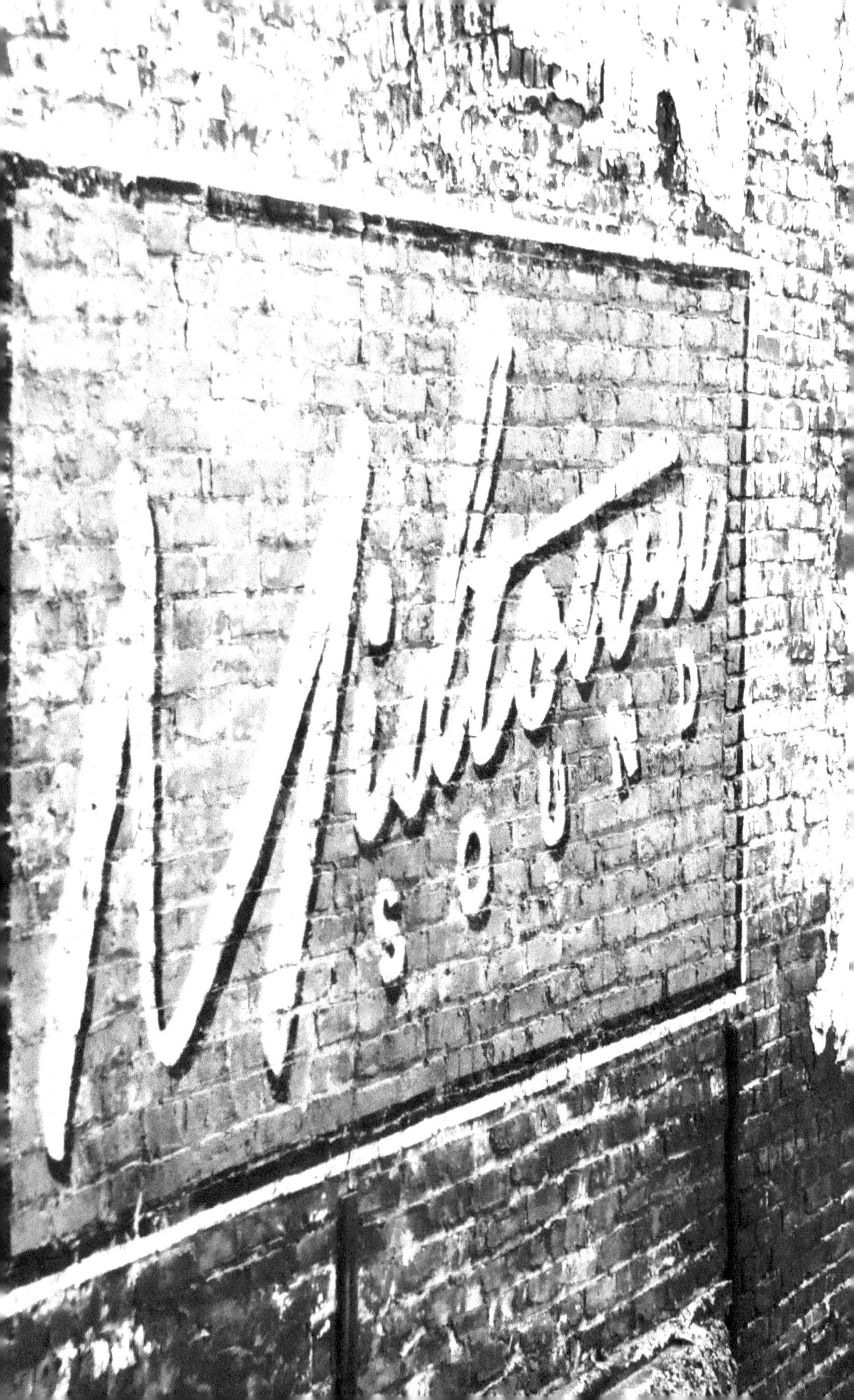
SOUP

LIKE THEN AND NOW

The first recorded music I listened to was on a reel-to-reel. It was the music of my parents and the music of the early seventies. There was a whole lotta groove and a little residual antiwar anthem in there also. We lived overseas, and people sent us homemade recorded reels. I loved that music. I loved to listen to it to the point of bugging the crap outta my parents. I bugged them so much they, with threats to my life to not screw anything up, taught me how to use the reel-to-reel myself. I loved the feel of threading the tape, running it over, around, and through the mechanics of the player much like threading a sewing machine. The machine itself had a hum to it, a smell to it that I cannot even begin to put to words. It really is one of those "if you know, you know" things.

Back in the States and the place I call home—Milwaukee, Wisconsin—the player was perched high up on some shelves between the dictionary on one side and a set of *Encyclopedia Britannica* on the other side. I would put the earphones on, slide down the wall, and listen to the music for hours. That was how I escaped my Cold War, bomb raid exercises, chain-smoking and alcoholic parents, Midwest (we had moved back to Wisconsin at this point), mostly good childhood.

Next, it was the record player. We'd slowly pull the LP out of the sleeve, careful to handle it by the edges only and gently put the pin of the direct drive motor into the center hole of the record. We'd place the needle onto the vinyl with a gentle hand, waiting for a few anticipatory seconds to hear the sound explosion. Hearing the first crackles of the record was the warm-up moan to the music that came shortly.

There is a little debate about which came first, the cassette or the eight-track, depending on your reference. My aunt Mary had an eight-track tape player and a box in the car carrying around a handful of those clunky tapes. My aunt was my first best friend. And like aunts the world over, she often got kid duty—me! My grandfather was a car guy, so she would borrow his car *du jour* and pick me up from school in some wicked rides! Her car wasn't too bad either! There was nothing in the world like driving around with my aunt, in her 1970-something Oldsmobile Cutlass 442 convertible on a summer evening. It was red, a little darker than candy-apple red, with a white leather interior that she managed to keep spotless, and with scalloped seat back cushions that I haven't seen since.

That car was really smokin', and to this day I still peruse the want ads, thinking by way of a fantasy, that maybe I'll buy one just like she had as a memento of some good times! She'd pop in a tape, and we sang our little hearts out! Then, in the middle of the best part of the song, it abruptly ended, and my aunt scrambled to put the next tape in. When it stopped, the silent music became the missing ingredient in that particular moment, and just like that, the moment was gone. It's like trying to recapture a lost sneeze, and if the stars were divinely aligned, if the temps were balmy and really suitable for a top-down convertible ride, not just wishful thinking in Wisconsin; if it was really good, it was like trying to recapture a lost orgasm.

Ahhhh . . . the cassette tape. The clicking of opening the case, a case that doubled as a windshield ice scraper in a pinch; the clicking of putting it in the player and then the clicking of the different buttons, record, play, rewind, rewind, play, stop. We made our mix tapes with cassette tapes. I called into the radio station and asked the DJ to play my favorite song. I waited for what seemed like forever, knowing it was at the end of a long list of everyone else's favorite songs. When it finally came on, I held a portable cassette player up to the speaker and held my breath at the same time, praying the phone didn't ring, no one came in my room, and no one yelled up the stairs for me. Mix tapes were our teenage angst anthem of choice. We had tapes of our fight songs, longing for love songs, and of course, broken heart songs. In some cases, it was a musical diary to which no one was privy. And if found, it was easily hidden in plain sight as "just some music" with no one the wiser.

Now, because of my particular love of music, I have it everywhere. I don't have to hold my breath for a perfect recording, I don't have to wait for the radio to play my favorite tune, and I don't worry about the tape becoming a mangled mess. My music is everywhere I want it to be. The warm-up to the listening experience may no longer be there; now it is an immediate immersion with streaming, my iTunes library, SiriusXM, and all other manner of binary replay. I am also rebuilding my LP collection, one $40 f***ing album at a time.

I miss the reel-to-reel. I do. Mostly because it was my first and is nostalgic. The eight-track leaves me with more questions than anything else, and I'm kinda meh about cassettes, though they are nostalgic as well.

There is not much today that has the umph of a teenage mixtape; the secret repository of crushes, the hyped-up blues of a broken heart, and the pain of trying to fit in. Albums have made a niche comeback, and I own a micro collection compared to what I used to have. I also have had CDs, iPods, and all manner of anytime, anywhere digital downloads. I'm quite curious about music in the next thirty years, and I will continue to enjoy my music from then and now.

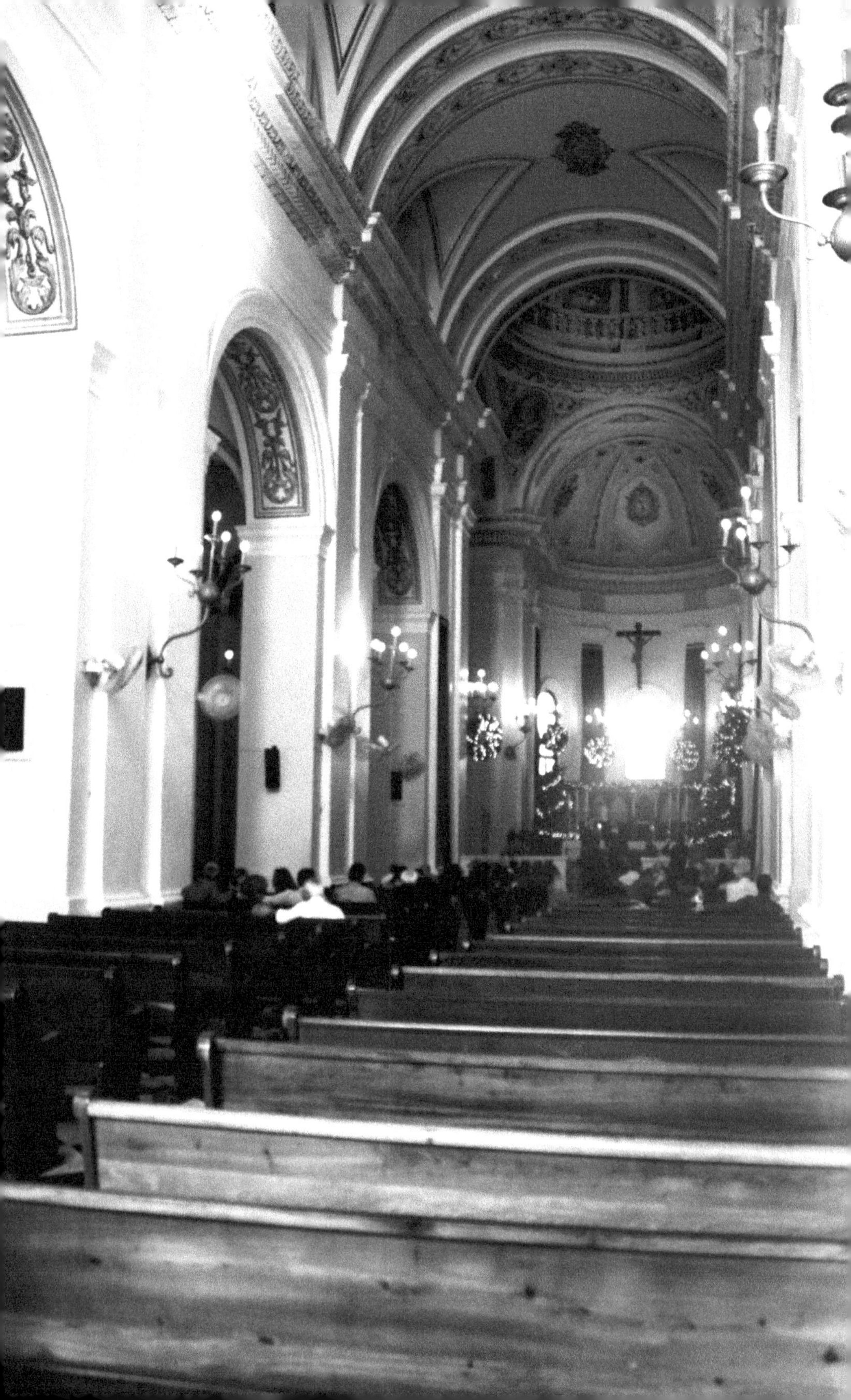

LOVE THY NEIGHBOR

Love thy neighbor as thyself. It's a great idea but not always so simple in application. It is easy to love somebody who is nice, easygoing, and thinks the same as you and has similar beliefs. But what about someone who is not so nice and completely different? Let's just start by saying that loving and liking are not the same thing! I can love someone, but I don't have to like them. One of the many definitions of *love*, according to Webster's, is "an affectionate concern for the well-being of others." The Buddhists I worked with in Northern India will end an email, a letter, or a post with, "May all sentient beings be well."

I live in Texas, and our governor just recently lifted our mask mandate. Those who disagreed with his decision got pretty ugly about it. He is wheelchair-bound, and people were saying things like, "Toss him out of his chair and throw it away, roll him down a hill and into a lake." I think you get the idea. I have bad asthma and personally will continue to wear a mask, but I would never wish ill will upon anyone who believes otherwise.

Can I love Hitler for the human being he was and the psychological trauma of bullying and rejection he endured as a young person? What about the kid who grows up in the ghetto seeing privilege all around him for everyone except himself and sees no way out other than being in a gang? Or the man who beats his kids because he was beaten as a child, and that is all he knows? I certainly don't have to like them, but can I love them for their humanity? As humans, we are all together on this big blue marble we call Earth. We are all trying to keep our heads above water, we are all trying to keep our families safe. So, to answer the question, "Can I love someone who is not so nice?" I'm trying.

My family used to toss about the expression, "Love thy neighbor as thyself." My question is this: How can I have love for someone else if I do not love myself? I know on some level, it looks like I do, but I don't; not if you look past the thinly veiled disguises of a new car, good relationship, and successful job. There, you might catch a glimpse of my truth. My self-talk is deprecating, demeaning, and destructive. I would NEVER let anyone else speak to me in such a manner, but somehow the insidious nature of self-talk has me letting the little nasties in. I tell myself, "You suck," "You're ugly," "You're too fat," "You're not good enough," "Who do you think you are?" I imagine I am not the only one. I think we all have our own version. No wonder the world is turned upside down (in my opinion). I really do think we are loving our neighbors as ourselves, and it ain't pretty.

Maybe if I truly loved myself, then loving my neighbor would be a non-issue. It would simply be an extension of my love for myself. Love does not discriminate between me or my neighbor. It doesn't choose, it just keeps on going. The thing about love is it grows when given away.

So just for today I'll practice loving myself and start by being kind to myself. Practice what you preach and what you teach your kids. I will practice what I tell my niece and nephew. Repeat after me: I am beautiful. I am deserving. I am smart. We really are, you know.

So spread the love and remind yourself and others who they are and what they can do. Remind them we really are an energetic bundle of love. Love never dies or goes away or becomes in short supply. We just stopped spreading it. As for me, I think I will spread love like my ego depends on it.

PLAY NICE

Dallas is quickly outgrowing its infrastructure regardless of how fast our city managers try to patch and expand things. At this point, playing catch-up is the most fruitless exercise in futility of which I can think. So at 6:30 on a nondescript Tuesday morning, I am in traffic.

If days of the week were children, Tuesday, Wednesday, and Thursday would be the collective middle child; Monday would be the eldest; and Friday, Saturday, and Sunday would be the collective youngest. Just like in *The Brady Bunch Movie*—the middle child, Jan, gets so completely exasperated about hearing all the parental praise showered on her older sister she cries out "Marcia, Marcia, Marcia!"—so too would the non-descript Tuesday cry out "Monday, Monday, Monday!" because Monday gets so much of our attention. Even on Tuesday, if it is particularly harried and chaotic, we hear people say, "It feels like a Monday." And this morning as I sit in traffic, it feels like a Monday morning!

So here I am, not so patiently sitting at a light to turn left. It's a two-lane left turn, and I'm in the outer lane. A pickup truck pulls up on my left, the inside of the two lanes; the one that has to make the tight left turn. These days pickups are all kinds of extra: extra big, extra long, extra gas-guzzling, and this particular truck is a "Texas Edition," so it has extra attitude.

Through the intersection is a little dotted line that delineates the two left turning lanes: an outside and an inside lane. As we make our way through the intersection and stay within our respective lines, I can choose the middle or far-right lane. The truck is relegated to the far-left lane only.

The light turns green, and I stay tight on the line, making my way into the middle lane and forcing the truck to stick to his assigned lane.

Aaannd there she is, that voice, *Play nice.*

"Good morning, Cinderella," I say to the voice in my head. I call her *Cinderella* this morning because she is living a fairy tale if she thinks I'm going to play nice. We are long past that point.

Mostly she sounds like my mother. Sometimes she sounds like my dad, and at other times, she is that committee of voices running commentary on so much of what I do these days.

This morning, I laugh and sarcastically say, "I know you," as I continue my way in to work. This drive is fraught with slow drivers, I-refuse-to-use-my-turn-signal drivers, speeding-up-getting-in-front-of-me-and-slowing-down-again drivers, and so many I'm-new-in-town drivers.

And so this morning is also fraught with a slew of out-loud profanities from me, an occasional brake check, refusing to let in the no-turn-signal people, and glaring dirty looks at the new-in-town people. I don't flip anyone off anymore since the last time I did that, the driver flashed a gun at me. I know! I know! You'd think I'd learn.

By now Cinderella has thrown her arms up in exasperation!

I just don't know what I'm going to do with you! That is definitely my mother's voice.

I am a firm believer in "you get what you give," so believe me when I say I had a crappy day at work! I began my day being inflexible, intolerant, rude, and demanding. That's what I gave at 6:30 in the morning, and that is exactly what I got All. Damn. Day. Long.

IT'S TIME TO GO

Hey baby, it's time to go now
We've been together a while
But you are contentious company
For now I have a field to plow
And demons to rid, old and vile
No longer bound by false Coventry
It's time to shed the weight of ages
That's found shelter in my soul
And heavies my heart along the way
Searching for my sages
It's time to let you go
Never to see the light of day
No longer yours to obligate
A different life to lead
I feel the weight of wings and feathers
A new hunger to sate,
A different appetite to feed,
Now loosened a hellish tether
Able to defy gravity
And finally free to fly
I'll go up, you go down
Freed of alternate depravity
And seeing beyond the sublime
I claim the wings and crown

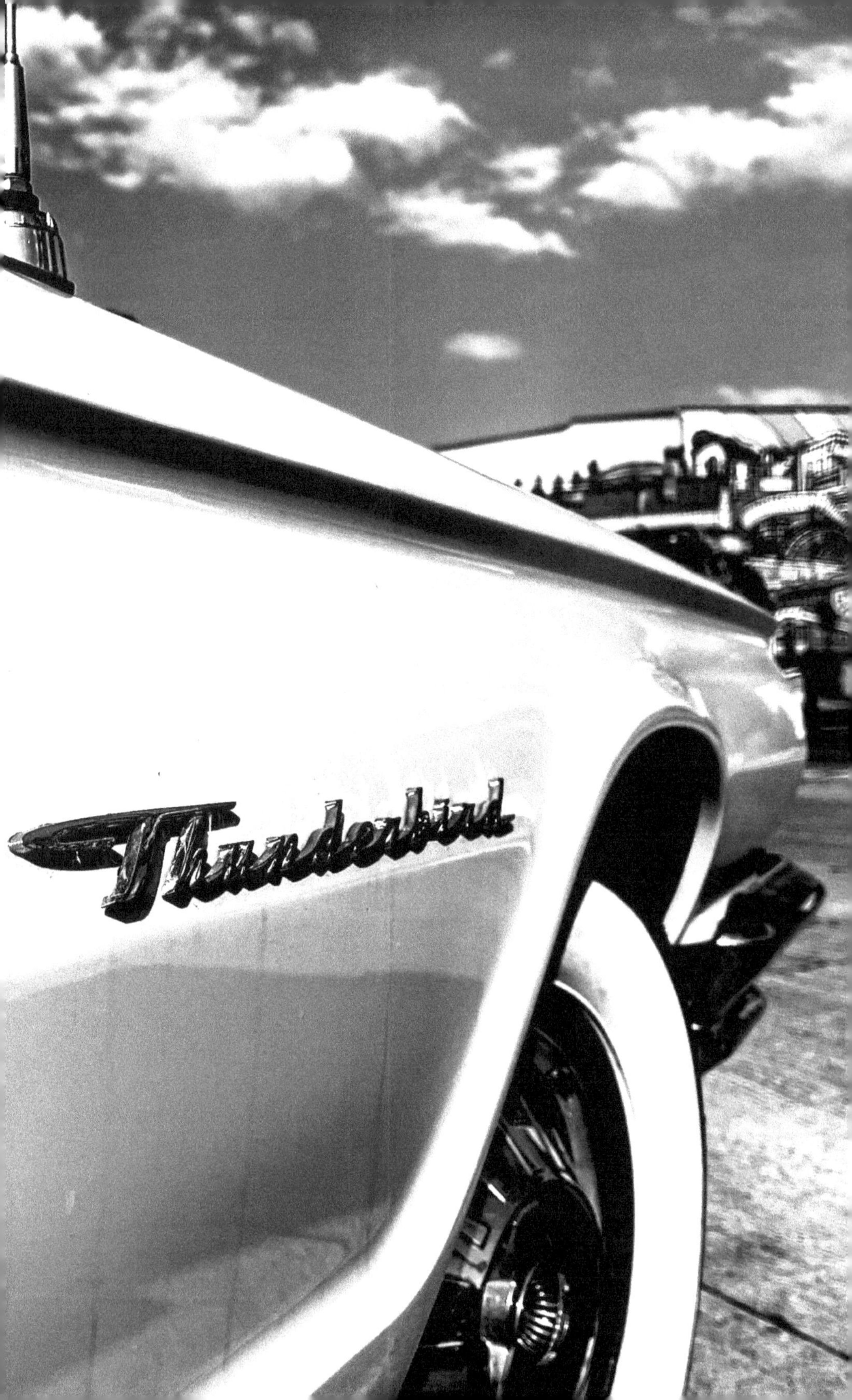

Thunderbird

THAT'S OKAY BABY

I am an occupational therapist in a large hospital. Somebody has to be my first patient of the day, and somebody has to be the last. For me and my ten-hour workday, it means the last person of the day is doing therapy at 5:00 or 5:30 p.m. The first one is usually at 8:00 in the morning. Not everyone fits neatly between 10:00 in the morning and 3:00 in the afternoon.

Most days I walk into a room and introduce myself. Most of the time I have to wake them up to do their therapy, and it is so very impolite first thing in the morning. I do try to be nice, though, but to those comfortable and asleep, my entry is inevitably an abrasive intrusion upon their slumbering souls. This morning is no exception. My first patient of the morning is in a drug-induced sleep, which requires a bit more effort to arouse. In the dark corner of the room, another body stirs on the couch and eventually stands up. Now I am apologizing profusely and wishing I had been more subtle when I walked into the room.

The visitor is probably fifty-five or sixty, though she looks like she might be seventy-five. I swear we met some thirty-five years ago while I was going to college in a small redneck Texas town that despite the university presence was still very conservative. Bubba and Boudreaux definitely outnumbered Beau and Buffy. I dropped out of school in the middle of my freshman year, then moved from the dorms to live in a singlewide and work at the local pizza place. I went from Texas A&M University to The School of Hard Knocks. I probably drank too much and ran with the people my mother warned me about. Thank God for growing up. The mystery lady from the couch in the corner could have very well been one of my running buddies from back then.

Her skin is tan and deeply wrinkled from what was probably lots of time in the sun and also probably lots of hard, physical work. It looks more like aged leather than actual skin. Her grin is wide and toothless, and the lines around her eyes deepen as her grin gets bigger. And that voice! That rough and raspy and gravelly voice with not an ounce of a feminine softness said, "That's okay, Baby."

It gets me. Every. Single. Time. Call me *baby* and I become putty; a malleable, mashable, emotional blob of nostalgia, and I have no clue where it comes from. But here's the catch and perhaps my prejudice, because not just everyone can call me Baby. It has to come from an older, poor, disenfranchised, socially tramped-on kind of person, typically from the South, who can still see the upside of things and really believes that life is good. These people don't usually have much, but they have family and faith, and they believe in their hearts they have enough.

Think about it. "That's okay, Baby" would not be the same coming from Queen Elizabeth or perhaps a bit closer to home, Maria Shriver or Rachel Madow. Oprah, maybe, but only because she had a rough beginning in her younger life. The same applies to other kinds of people. Old Black men with weathered skin, deeply lined faces, and hair so white it's truly devoid of color: they can call me Baby. Old white men wearing faded overalls that drive beat-up old

It gets me every single time. Call me baby and I become putty, a malleable, mashable, emotional blob of nostalgia. But there's a catch...

pickups from the sixties and who say very little, if anything at all can call me Baby. And worn-out, run down, faith-filled Black women that have raised three generations, worked two jobs, and cooked tons of food for scores of people, who don't have much, but love life despite the struggles and obstacles thrown at them, them too! All of them. They can call me Baby.

My grandfather died a wealthy man. Though he began life quite modestly, I always knew him as a pretty rich guy. Now before you get excited and think I'm buying the next round, it all went to his next wife. He got reclusive as he got older and wealthier. He bought a new Cadillac every two years and built his fences higher and higher, both physical and emotional. He never seemed happy with his life and with the things money brought him. And he would have *never* said, "That's okay, Baby."

Don't Stop Believin   · Journey
Car   · Tracy Chapman
Sleep While I drive   Melissa Ethridge
Feeling   · Boston
· Queen
· Stevie Wonder
Rain - The Judds
Etheridge
TDK
DYNAMIC PERFORMANCE
ON BASIC CONSTRUCTION CASSETTE
D1/TYPE I

MIX TAPE

The food delivery driver showed up an hour and fifteen minutes late for lunch, short of breath, frazzled, and with blond hair going every which way, much like his energy. He says he is having a terrible day; traffic is horrible, there is so much construction, and the restaurants are running late. That's why my lunch is late. After his monologue of reasons for his bad day, he thrusts my order at me and says, "But you have a great day." There is a bit of a Mona Lisa-esque tone to his voice, so I don't quite know how to take it. Sincere or sarcastic? I walk away, now grumpy myself, and really hungry. As I go back upstairs, I'm muttering, "Traffic? Really? It's Dallas, dude! Construction? Really? Again, it's Dallas, dude! IT'S DALLAS!" The construction crane has replaced our state bird!

Now on automatic pilot, I sit down after lunch to write my notes for the morning. Per my usual, I put my headset in and press play on my iPod. There are a thousand or more songs on my iPod, and I hit shuffle. Included in my playlists is a "mix tape" for my mom, "Mom's Mix." Much like Chris Pratt's character, Peter Quill, in *Guardians of the Galaxy*, my mom is gone, and I am attached to these songs for sentimental reasons. They are songs that take me back to a different time. A time when a bad day was running out of Apple Jacks and not being able to get the rabbit ears to pull in a good signal on the TV. They are days of sit-down dinners, homemade meals, no box or can involved, and music playing on the reel-to-reel. They are days of my mom laughing and healthy and struggling to corral her rambunctious kids. The mix is full of sixties, seventies, and eighties musicality. Mom also loved ragtime, classical, and elevator music. The elevator music, though, is conspicuously missing from Mom's Mix!

Still on automatic pilot, I type away for the better part of thirty minutes, and in that time six to seven songs play. The music plays in the background and keeps the hustle and bustle of the world around me from invading my thoughts. Every now and then the songs present me to something bigger, reminding me of the vastness and intimacy of life. For real! I come off automatic as I hear things will get better, a message coming through my headset by way of the song "O-O-H Child" by The Five Stairsteps, and I think, *YES, they are!* Not because my life is horrible, but because I have gotten myself into a crappy mood and want out.

The next song to play from Mom's Mix is "Beautiful Noise" by Neil Diamond, her not-so-secret crush. It's a song about the noise of city life, the noise of being busy, the noise people make when in a bad mood, and how all that noise really can be beautiful. It is the noise of life, and life does not care if that noise makes us happy or sad.

So my delivery driver was just making noise. And in that space, I can appreciate him feeling like Sisyphus, always going uphill, always getting near the top just to fall back again and again, never getting to the other side. The coworker who snapped at me? Just noise, beautiful noise. The couple who is arguing? Just noise, beautiful noise. There is a hum to life, a mutual melody, a shared pulse that inextricably connects us, whether stranger or sibling. I am reminded we are all part of a much larger narrative, a universal opus that transcends generations, race, and sex. Our skin and opinions may be of a different color, but we all bleed red. We all breathe the same air, and all succumb to gravity. So for a moment, anyway, I heard all the complaints, criticisms, and concerns in the space of a beautiful noise, in the space of a universal ache, a universal want for something beautiful to emerge. All of that is the symphony of all of us. And each of us is a different instrument in the orchestra of life. The music, the song, and the narrative that's created are the same. It is the sound of One. Maybe next time I can get the beautiful noise to last a day, then a week, then a year, then a lifetime. Goals, people!

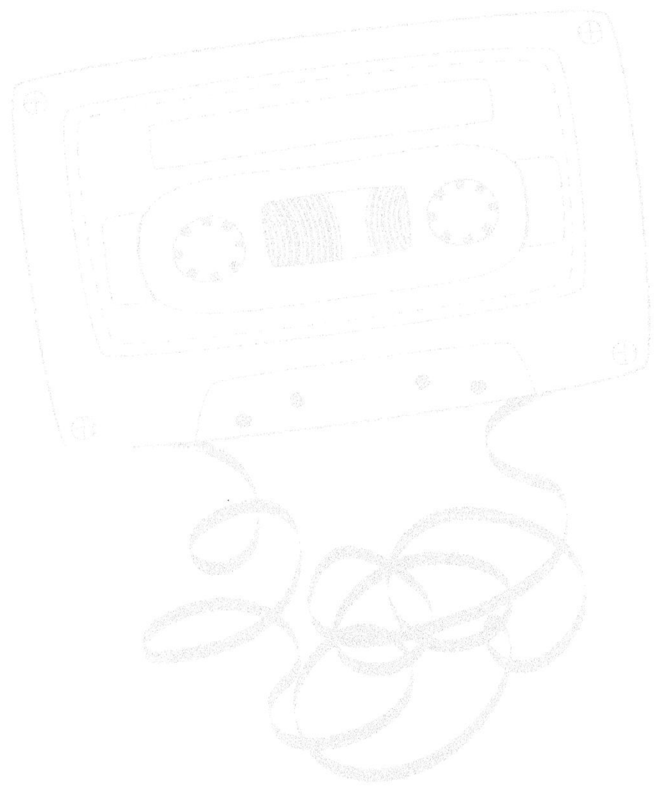

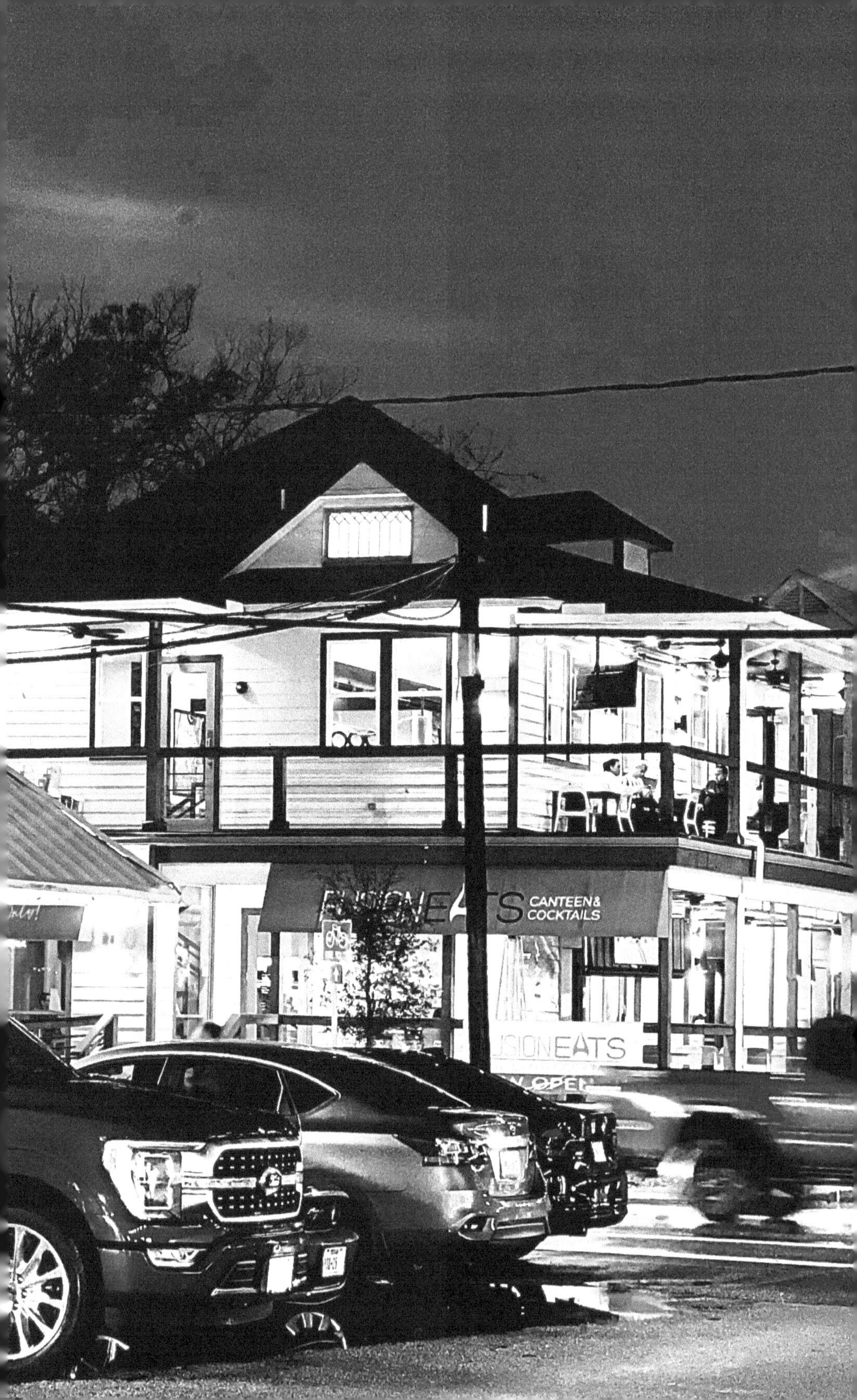

FUSIONEATS CANTEEN & COCKTAILS
FUSIONEATS
OPEN

HOMOGENIZED

I went to see my doctor for a checkup. His last name is Sullivan, and I found myself wondering where he was from. With a name like Sullivan, I'm guessing England? Ireland?

Turns out, it's Irish.

Sullivan is the third most common last name in Ireland and the ninety-second most common last name in the States. I knew I liked him, and now I like him even more. I have an affinity for that part of the world. A small slice of my ancestral pie is Scottish. Not the same as Irish, I know, but close enough for me. I am a mutt, pure Heinz 57. I cannot say I am Polish, German, Irish, Scottish, or Russian. I am all of them. And I am none of it anymore. I am like a painting where all the colors have run together, and you can't tell the original painting from the blurred mess of color. I miss not having any connections to my ancestral past. Instead of being a beautiful watercolor painting by Monet or Wyeth, I feel more like the disconnected, surrealistic art of Picasso.

During COVID 2020, my sister and I felt a little beat-up and battle-weary as the pandemic raged on and forced changes in both our lives. She lost a job and was having quite a difficult time finding another one. What was even harder for her was rewriting her identity without one. I had a job, working at a large hospital where I watched people die, indiscriminately, from COVID. The year 2020 was the year the Grim Reaper came disguised as

COVID, and if you worked in healthcare, you saw behind the hood. I know I did.

My sister and I don't live in the same city or even the same region of the state, so she drove north, and I drove south. We met in the middle and brought our collective and epigenetic grief with us, because, when you grieve, it's not just that one thing. It's everything. All over again. Past. Present. And future.

We found a local pub and crawled in to lick our wounds. At some point, the owner came over to make sure we were enjoying ourselves, and in short order, we were winding our conversational threads into a Technicolor coat of familial background with him. As it happened, he was a genealogical *NUT* as much as my sister. And in another short order, we were winding our way through the pub to his office, where we talked about all things ancestral. He showed us maps, pulled up pages on the internet, and shared his own personal family documents. My eyes glazed over, but my sister was in her element and so completely tickled to have found a kindred spirit. It wasn't long before it surfaced that we were McCalls. On my father's side. By way of his mother.

Our genial pub owner exclaimed, "Y'all are McCalls? Y'all are crazy!"

And I wondered to what we owed that particular stereotypical assignment. Turns out it is nothing more than centuries of storytelling. The McCall clan is pretty diluted these days compared to our tartan-wearing, crest-bearing days.

My sister and I are also a little German, Polish, and even Russian-Jewish. Some of my family were Jewish people who fled Odessa. Which time? I don't know. That little gem was superficially hidden when my Catholic great-grandmother divorced Morris Herschberger, her gambling, boozing, Jewish husband. She then reclaimed her maiden name, and in doing so, procured some degree of safety for herself and my grandfather-to-be. It was not a good idea to be Jewish in Milwaukee around the early 1900s, even in name only.

Anything cultural, ancestral, anything Jewish is long, long gone. There are no more traditions, habits, or holidays. The only Jewish holdover that survived the dilution and homogenization of my family tree was an occasional *oy vey, putz, schmuck*, and *schlep*. That's it, folks; just a few, choice words.

When my Polish maternal grandmother was alive, she made spaetzle, Polish sausage, red cabbage, pierogi, and cabbage rolls. Her last name was Kwasneski, shortened to Kwas later as immigrants tried to hide their origins by way of a telltale last name. Kwasneski was as telling as Herschberger, and both got sacrificed on the altar of the American dream. And thus began the dilution of this branch of the family tree.

Most people know me as a Valentine; most assume it's Italian. Our version of Valentine is German and was altered as my relatives came through Ellis Island because the current version is much easier for Americans to pronounce than the German version. And so began the homogenization of that particular branch.

While my family history is a rich, colorful, and textured tapestry, I feel like a diluted and watered-down version of all of it where nothing stands out. When my grandparents were alive, there were a handful of old-world holdouts that showed up during holidays and big family celebrations. Those traditions died with them.

I've been told to make my own traditions. It's not as simple as that. I miss a sense of connection to something larger that, on one hand, is familiar, even if only vague at times. Those crazy McCalls are still kicking, and though homogenized, I doubt they've completely assimilated. It's been more than twenty years since I have seen those cousins, but my sister visited the McCall girls a few years back. They now have families and kids of their own. No more tartan or kilts.

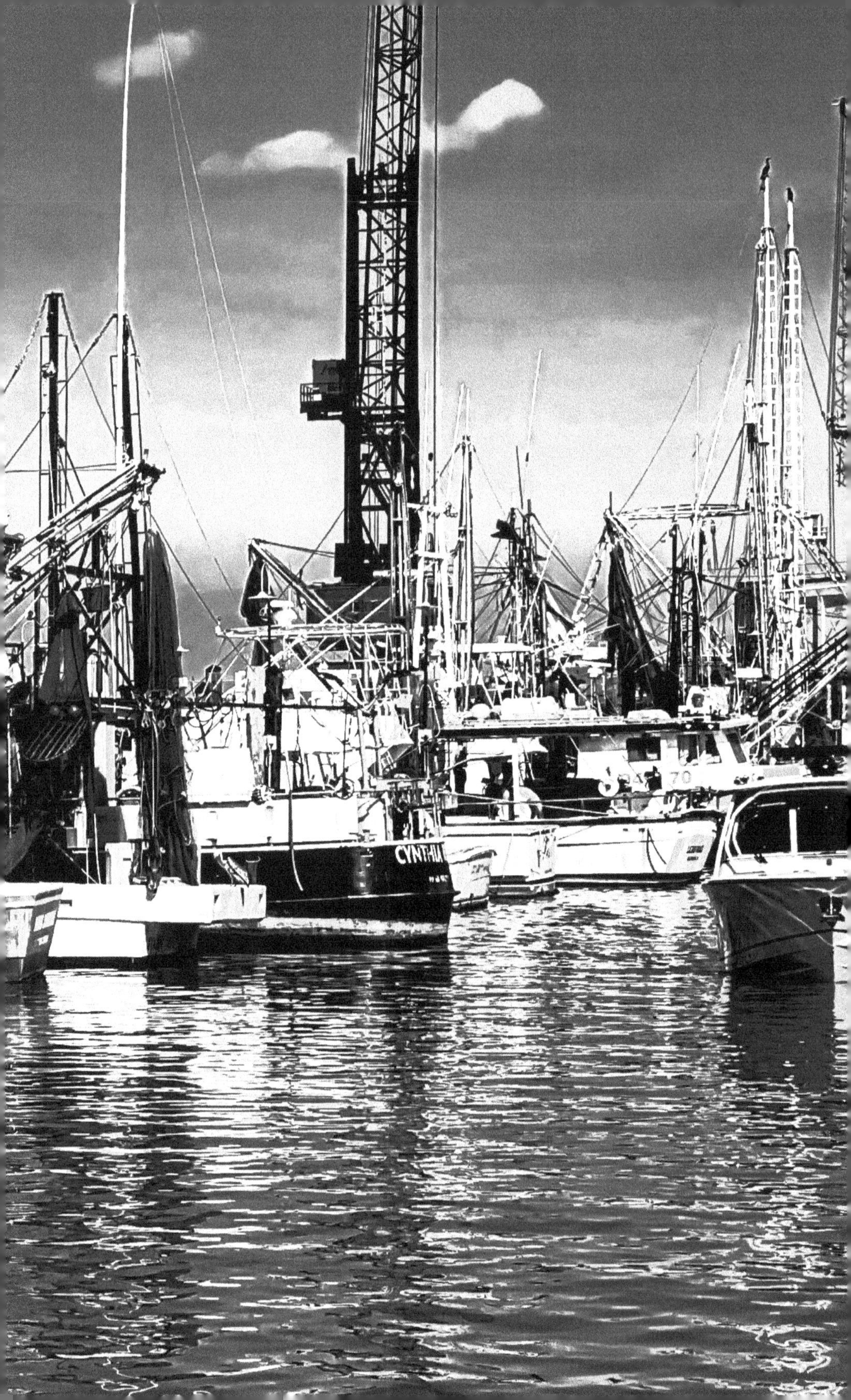

BAD MOOD

The beauty of the city waking up against the burgeoning pastel pink and orange sky is something by which to be inspired. It is an artist's palette for sure. The city lights still twinkle in the waning darkness as the night languishes in a final stretch, and the sun ascends, dancing with the moon in the rising dawn. From all angles, it is a gorgeous day. There are no clouds, no traffic. The temp is chilly, worthy of my favorite sweatshirt, and it's supposed to warm up to seventy-five degrees, perfect for my favorite shorts. It really does not get much better than this.

Despite the perfection of this morning, a darkness brewing in my mood threatens to spill over the edges of decency. It is very much like when I forget to empty yesterday's coffee pot before brewing a new one.

The mixture of lukewarm, stale, mud-like, take-the-enamel-off-your-teeth coffee spills over the pot and seeps out, spreading cold over the marble counter with a familiar but unpleasant smell about it. Like the darkness that heavies my mood, it spreads, smelly and making a mess of things around it. My current state of mind, like the coffee, spills out also. It seeps into the nooks and crannies where the bits of a good mood remain, desperately trying to survive.

So here I am, bewildered by the beguiling beauty of the new day, yet soaked to the bone with the pervasiveness of a bad mood; a bad mood that defies explanation, begs the white flag of surrender, and perhaps, even an emotional hazmat suit.

TENDER-HEARTED

To all my tender-hearted people, you who bring the light, who hold the doors open and create opportunity, fight for good to prevail, love until it hurts and weep until you are dry, I see you. For those of us who wear our hearts on our sleeves for all the world to see and leave our "door mats" out for all the world to use, I know you. For us who create beauty from ugliness and love deeply, unabashedly; who live our lives as an art installation, exposing our hearts to the criticisms, judgments, and brutality of humanity; I am you. Remember, we are the ones the world needs! If cold is an absence of heat, and dark an absence of light, ugliness an absence of beauty, and evil the absence of good, then we declare ourselves the conveyors of truth, creators of beauty, and purveyors of light. We are the torches that hold bright for humanity. The people of the world don't know it, but they need us! I, for one, am willing to be IT, the one that stands for beauty, for the brightness of humanity, and for what IT means to be a good person!

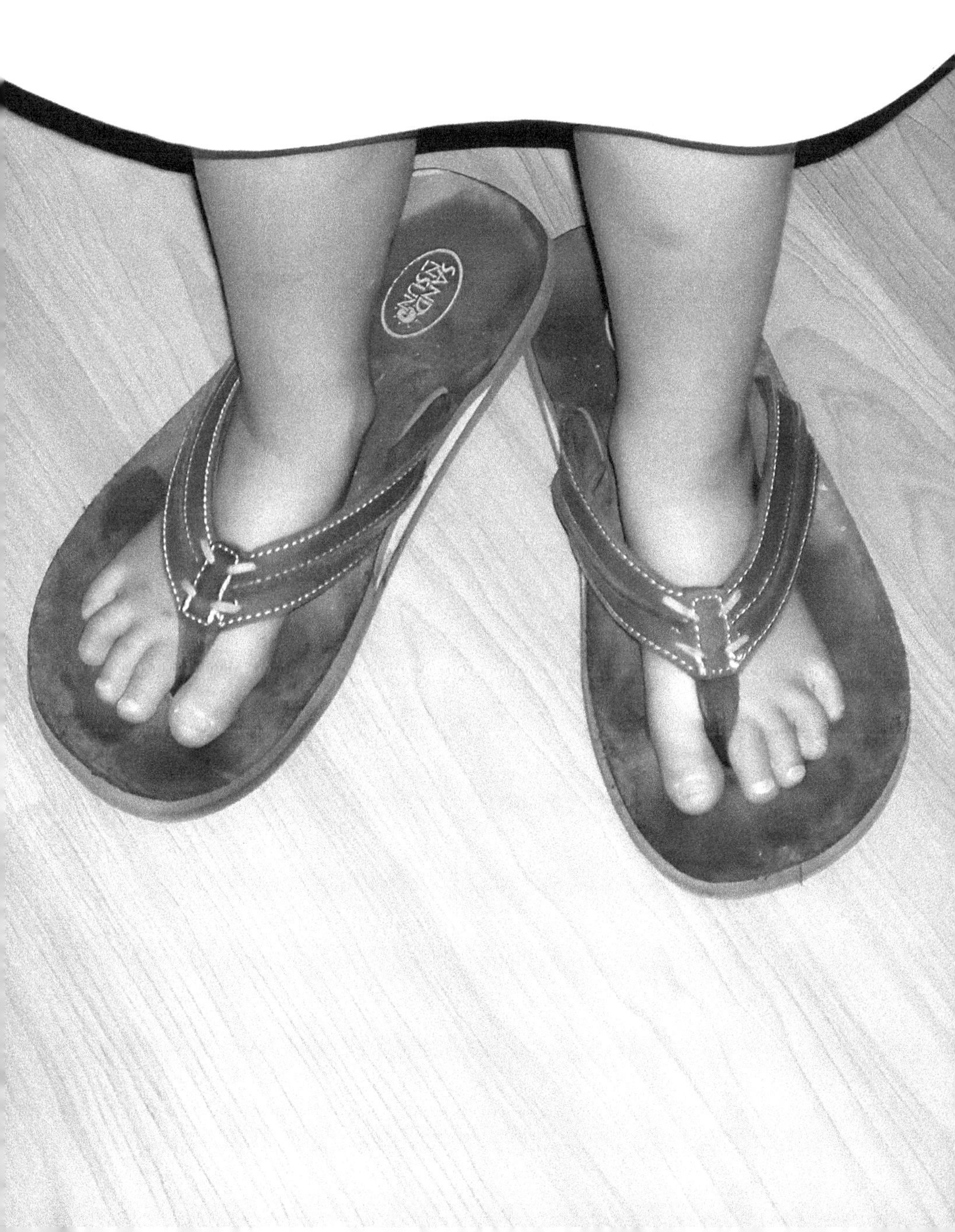

SAND
&SUN

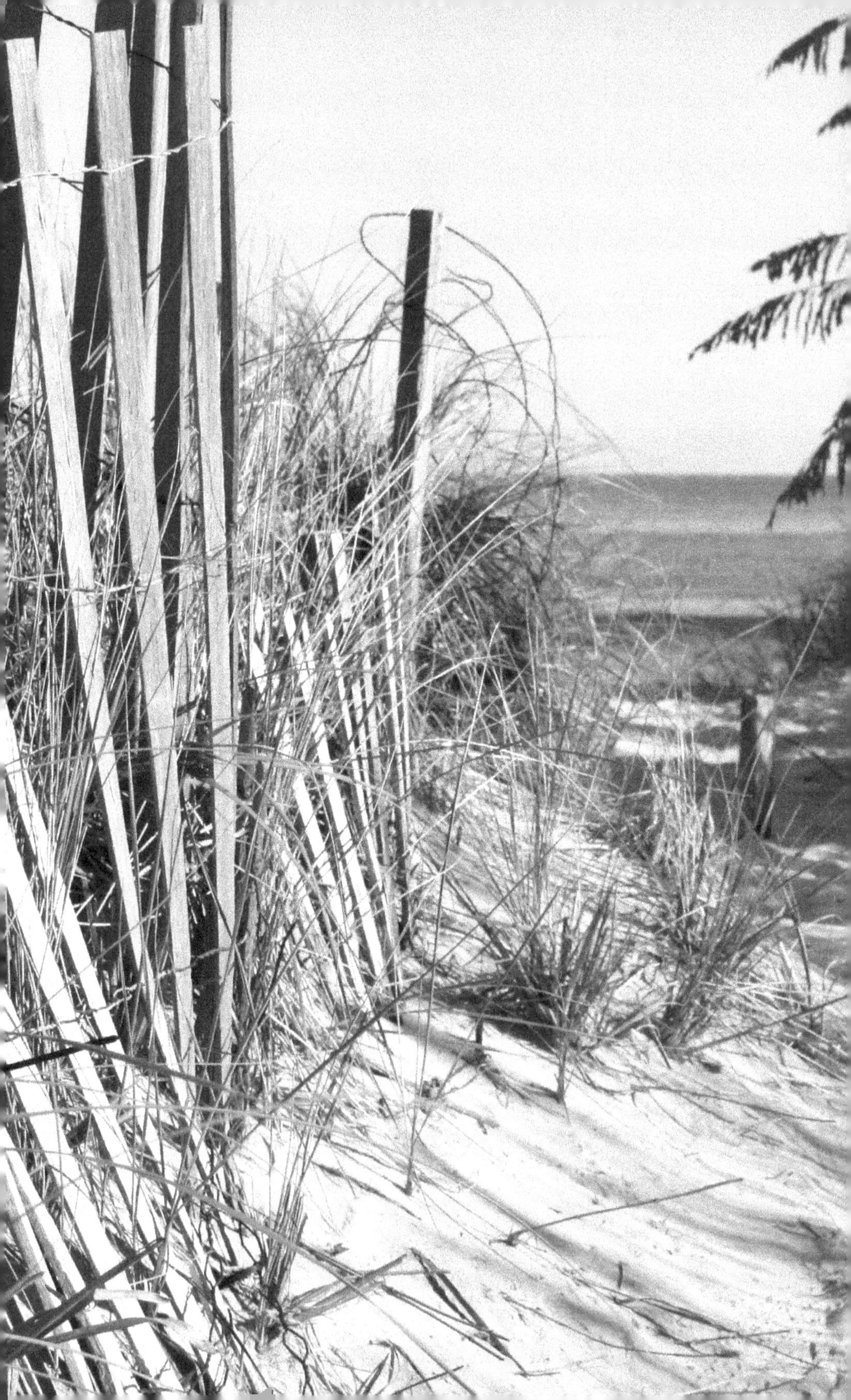

GEMINI ROOTS

Constitutionally, there is nothing about me that is remotely a hippie. Okay, maybe a little. I believe I am more Victorian, though, and to be more precise, more like a royal in jeans and a t-shirt than a hippie in heels and formal wear. This is the duality of Gemini, the two-sided nature, the *A-* and *B* side.

My *A* side loves a fancy table and knows the difference between a salad, dessert, and entrée fork. I know the difference between all the different spoons and glasses and have impeccable manners when I choose to pull them out of my ass. I miss going to fancy restaurants. When I do go, I get dressed up and feast like a queen.

My *B side*, in turn, is so uncomfortable at having to sit up straight and keep my elbows off the table, I hurry home to get back into my sweatpants and t-shirt. I then wonder what exactly I was missing because the absence of casual comfort and the presence of pretentiousness were painfully palpable. I'll inevitably repeat this process in six months or a year when the experience fades, and the fantasy fuels some vague memory, perhaps even a memory of a previous lifetime.

I am a Gemini. Geminis are supposed to be extroverted, fun, adventurous, adaptable, social butterflies, and curious. While I am very curious and tend not to stick to one book, topic, or project, I am ALSO introverted, like things my way, and am not freewheeling. I was once even called "a stick-in-the-mud" In my defense, I was dragged to a party after a root canal with people I didn't know, on pain meds that made me sick, and with an ex who didn't give a shit.

I am a social butterfly, but only with a very small group of friends. Get me outside of that group, and I become shy and quiet. And I'm adventurous, but not in a drop-everything-and-go kinda way. I like to know where I am going, and I do know the most thought-out plans change. I like order, symmetry, patterns, and some degree of matching. I like manners, politeness, and standing on ceremony. I look before I leap and always look before I cross the road.

There is one caveat, though. Say, "I dare you," and something flips in my brain. I am no longer shy and quiet. I become this creature, larger than life, an *f*-you to boundaries and all common sense, tempting fate and making my parents' hair gray. They say Geminis are indecisive. Well, this is about the only time I become decisive, and it is fueled by the winds of fate. I got a tattoo, bungee jumped off a perfectly good bridge, and dove forty feet into a cenote—a deep, natural well where the earth around it collapsed—because someone said, "I dare you."

I have had one joint replaced (about to have the other one replaced), torn up my knee, dislocated my shoulder, broke my arm, and have had several concussions. I don't need a dare. I need an off switch.

I once told a friend that I was easygoing "like water off a duck's back." I think she choked. Like really. Good thing I know how to do the Heimlich. As for me, it was probably some bit of deep-seated knowing of what a Gemini should be and a whole lot of wishful thinking.

Over time, I have learned to adjust and be flexible. I've learned that to go with the flow is a helluva lot easier than trying to swim upstream. I have also learned that setting boundaries is not necessarily "my way or the highway" but rather is an act of self-love. Although, to those who are not good for me, boundary-making appears as "my way or the highway." Funny how that works.

True to my Gemini sign, the sign of the twins, I have two sides. I must be the twin the books don't tell you about, the *B* side. Kris is also a Gemini. She is all the things I am not and vice versa. She is the *A* side to my *B* side. And it is all part of my Gemini roots.

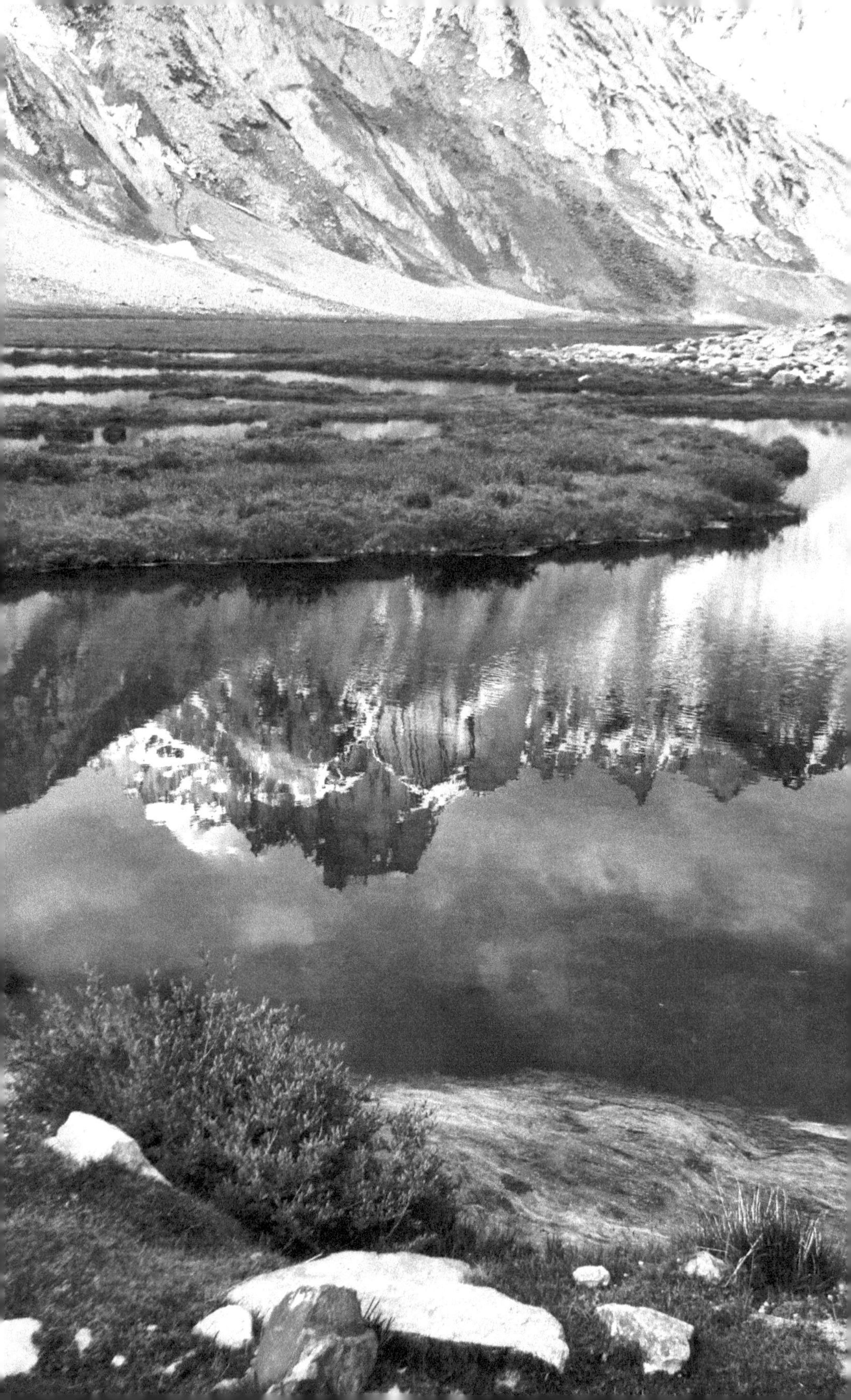

LOST AND FOUND AT THE SAME TIME

A friend of mine used the phrase "lost and found at the same time" to describe Anthony Bourdain, chef, reality TV star, world traveler, and his immersion into foreign culture and cuisine. On the one side, he was a departure from the homogenized American suburb and a deep dive into the culture wherever he was; he allowed himself to be "found," feeling at home and in love with the people there. On the other side, he was lost, because the country and the culture were simply different from his own.

The idea of being lost and found at the same time resonated with me, bringing with it that sense of timeless familiarity, the feeling that something is so familiar and known it crosses years and generations and leaves a sense of being so comfortably settled. We have all had those well-known and worn times of feeling "lost and found at the same time." The angst of being a teenager left me there, as did the angst of my twenties and all those times I was emotionally lost, I was really lost and found at the same time. Probably more found than lost, now that I can look back on all of it.

I received a birthday wish from one of my cousins. Growing up, she was my go-to, the one I thought was super cool, and the one I wanted to be like. I wanted to be friends, but the gap in our ages was big enough to make me "just a kid" for a long time. We moved away, and in this way, I was lost. Our relationship was lost.

Years later, when she said, "Happy birthday," I replied with "Thanks! I miss you." Her response was very simple, "I miss you too, honey." Suddenly, I was found. I just started crying: a lot. I was lost in the memories of my childhood, of us, of my affection for her, and of my love for a cousin that, in this moment, closed the gap of drifting apart. I was found again in the warmth and love and embrace of family. In a moment, I was lost and found at the same time.

My parents divorced after nearly thirty years, my dad falling victim to the sirens, unable to look away and not strong enough to resist their voice, and cheated on my mom. The ink had barely dried on their divorce papers when my mom died. My life tumbled, free-falling into a world of uncertainty and circling the drain of lostness, finally plunging into an abyss, dark and without direction and seemingly without an end. I floundered for a few years, feeling very lost.

I stopped eating. I couldn't work. But eventually, I did get found. Being found implies returning to something familiar. At first, nothing seemed familiar in a world without Mom. But then I found little familiar things. The plant on my balcony. My favorite TV show. My neighbor smiling at me. After a while, the uncharted waters of my new reality became more and more familiar.

My sister and I recovered from our parents' divorce and the death of our mom. What I did find, though, was that I was navigating uncharted waters, which with time became familiar. And when enough time passed, the feeling of being found loosely settled over me. During this period, I felt a sense of being lost and found at the same time.

My life now is very independent of my parents. The foundation being laid, my parents have less and less of a pivotal role in the person I am today. The same can be said for many others: the ex that cheated, the boss that fired me for no reason, and so on. I am the captain of this ship I call my life. Her crew and I are sailing on, now welcoming the uncharted, unnavigated, sometimes choppy future ahead with full knowledge, I am lost and found at the same time. Lost in acceptance of what is and what isn't, lost in family, lost in adventure, lost in faith, lost in surrender. And because found implies being returned to something familiar, I am always returned to love.

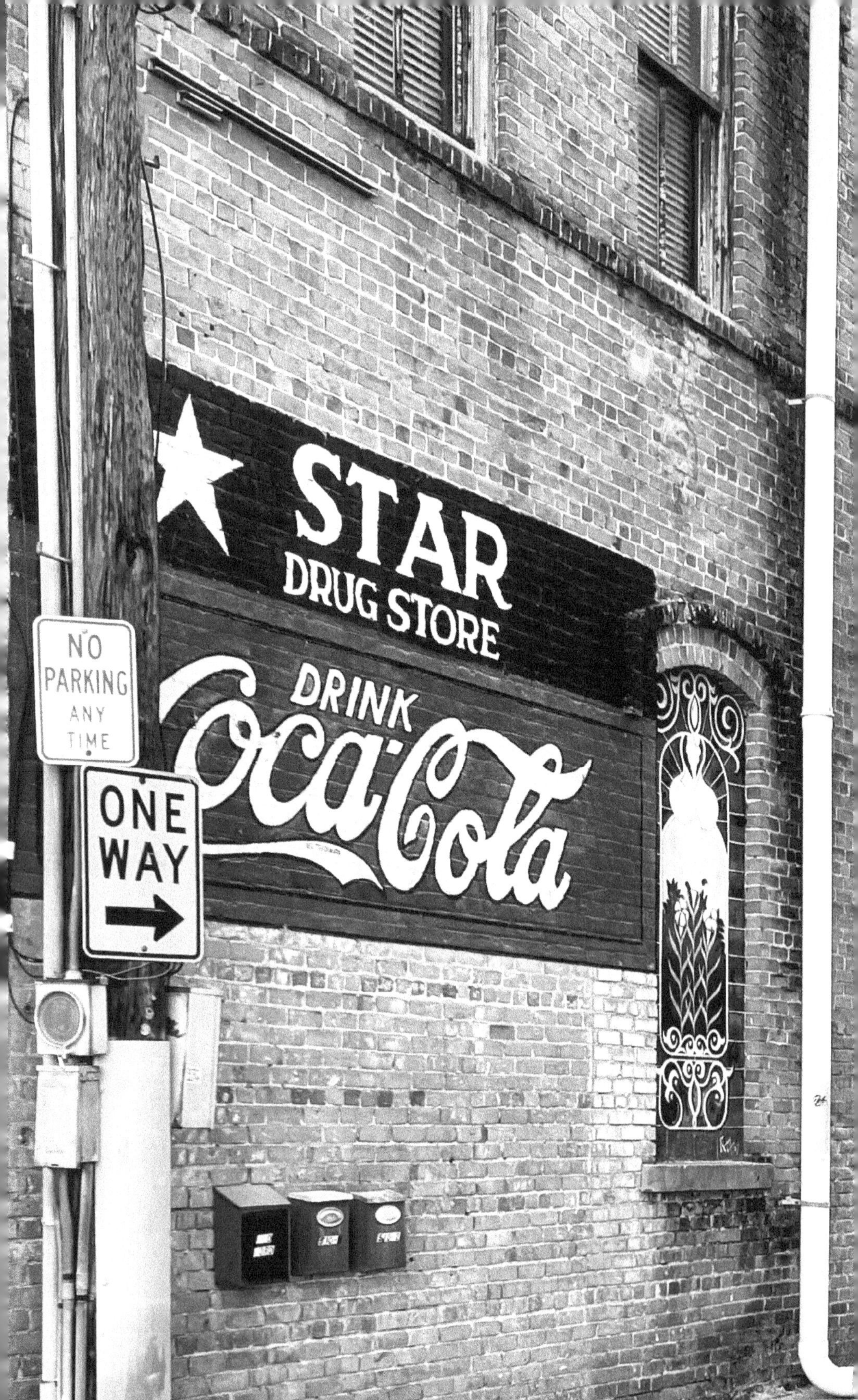
STAR
DRUG STORE
DRINK
Coca Cola
NO
PARKING
ANY
TIME
ONE
WAY

JUST DOING HIS THING

I am waking up this morning tired and sore from a weekend so busy it left me looking forward to going back to work. Now that I say this, truthfully, I'd rather be sitting in my corner of the couch reading a good book and sipping coffee so strong my heart flutters like a butterfly hungrily looking for the next flower. I find myself waiting for the sun to peek through some emerging storm clouds—actual storm clouds and metaphorical ones as well. Faster and faster the clock ticks, so I get up and stagger about my semi-dark apartment, my bones aching and spirit weary.

I make my way into work, a little late but still within the window to clock in and be on time. It is now rush hour at the hospital as the night shift leaves and the morning shift arrives. My elevator finally arrives; I get in and of course, per Murphy's Law, it gets held up at the last second by one of the kitchen staff. I have to share my elevator with all this coming and going of the morning rush hour as the window to clock in is ready to slam shut on me. The other guy in the elevator is pulling two large, lumbering, not–moving–fast–at–all carts of breakfast trays. I recognize him. He is always working, always smiling, always happy. The carts he pulls are cumbersome; ten times bigger than he and difficult to control. He has *two* of them.

Getting into the elevator with these two carts is a logistically painful process to observe, much like trying to park a Ford F-250 in a crowded parking lot, in the last remaining spot left that says "compact only." I am getting more irritated with each deafening tick of my watch. Tick. Tick. Tick. Finally across the elevator threshold and free to do something else other than concentrate on herding those carts, he looks at me, grins big, and raises one hand in salutation. His English is broken and thick with an accent of an Asian variety as he heartily and earnestly says, "GOOD MORNING, GOOD MORNING!" And he means it! Like a good belly laugh, it comes from deep within, emerging as authentic, genuine, and unencumbered of any hidden meaning. It is a pure, clean wish of well-being not often seen in today's world of clocks, meetings, and a near-constant deluge of distractions.

And yeah, ya know what? It really is a good morning!

It is all rather ironic, really. I was irritated and watching what I thought was a mild, slow-motion disaster unfolding before me. Turns out it was just a guy doing his thing. And inside of doing his thing, he took one of those precious seconds to wish me good morning . . . and I almost missed it.

I almost missed the simple beauty of another human being and almost let the beauty of an emerging day—one unencumbered of any hidden agenda—sneak past me.

IT'S A JOB

Working at the hospital was a whole new level of extra during COVID. We were all used to hearing a code blue called. Unfortunately, it is part of where we work, part of the job, and to some degree, it is part of working at a hospital. Fortunately for me and my sissy heart, I am never part of a code blue. We have a team of people with the hearts of lions and the fortitude of warriors for that.

As big as the hospital is, we do not hear the codes daily or even weekly. And as big as we are, we don't get many veterans either. But at times the VA hospital gets full, and we get their overflow. Other times a vet is brought in by ambulance because we are the closest hospital.

COVID was a game changer. I really do not care what your beliefs about COVID are. I'm not even sure what I think or feel about it. But real people were really dying. And for some, if they didn't die, they wished they had because the life they had leaving the hospital was a wispy shadow of the life they had before going in.

I am an occupational therapist, and in the middle of COVID, I was just trying to do my job. We went from an almost 1,000-bed hospital with sometimes zero code blues per day to about a 1,500-bed hospital with three to four codes called in a single day. Normally, all the rooms are single-bed rooms. During COVID, multiple units went to double-bed rooms, and our emergency department added more pods. A pod has multiple rooms but is smaller than a floor unit, also known as a ward. We were initially pods *A* through *R*. But during COVID, pod *Z* was a tent in the ER parking lot.

As numb as we are to hearing codes, I don't think I will ever become numb to hearing up to three and four in a day. And that does not even count the ones in the intensive care unit (ICU), because all those codes were handled internally by the ICU team, and unless you worked in that particular ICU, you would never know a code happened.

I will never unsee a resident physician straddling a patient in the bed, doing CPR. It is so much more violent than anything on TV. With every compression, the patient's body moves like a rag doll. I will also never forget the number of vets that died at our hospital. Because they were veterans, it was paged overhead, "May I have your attention, please. May I have your attention, please. Today a United States Veteran has died in our hospital. We will have a moment of silence for the next sixty seconds." And then the silence. But not just any kind of silence. It was a heavy, punctuated silence that served as a moment to recognize a soul among souls who volunteered to put his or her life on the line for a country of strangers. They were given a moment of silence for a lifetime of service. Kris, my wife, said in her hospital, all available staff lined the hall when they got the announcement that a vet had passed. I wish the veterans got a "go past go for free" card. And with COVID, I wish the rest of us got a "get out of jail free" card.

I never imagined I would be in that situation as a healthcare worker. The death was unimaginable. The suffering was impossible.

Now, with most restrictions all but gone from our daily lives, I still go to work. It is still a job. I don't hear many codes anymore, and the units that were turned into closed-off COVID wards are back to normal. But none of *us* are back to normal. Some much less than others. There are many who have left healthcare and many more with varying degrees of PTSD. I really have come to dislike the term "new normal." Dare I say I hate the expression. I hate it because I refuse, I refuse to settle for the way we are being forced to let go of the way things were. Maybe I just refuse to settle as an act of defiance.

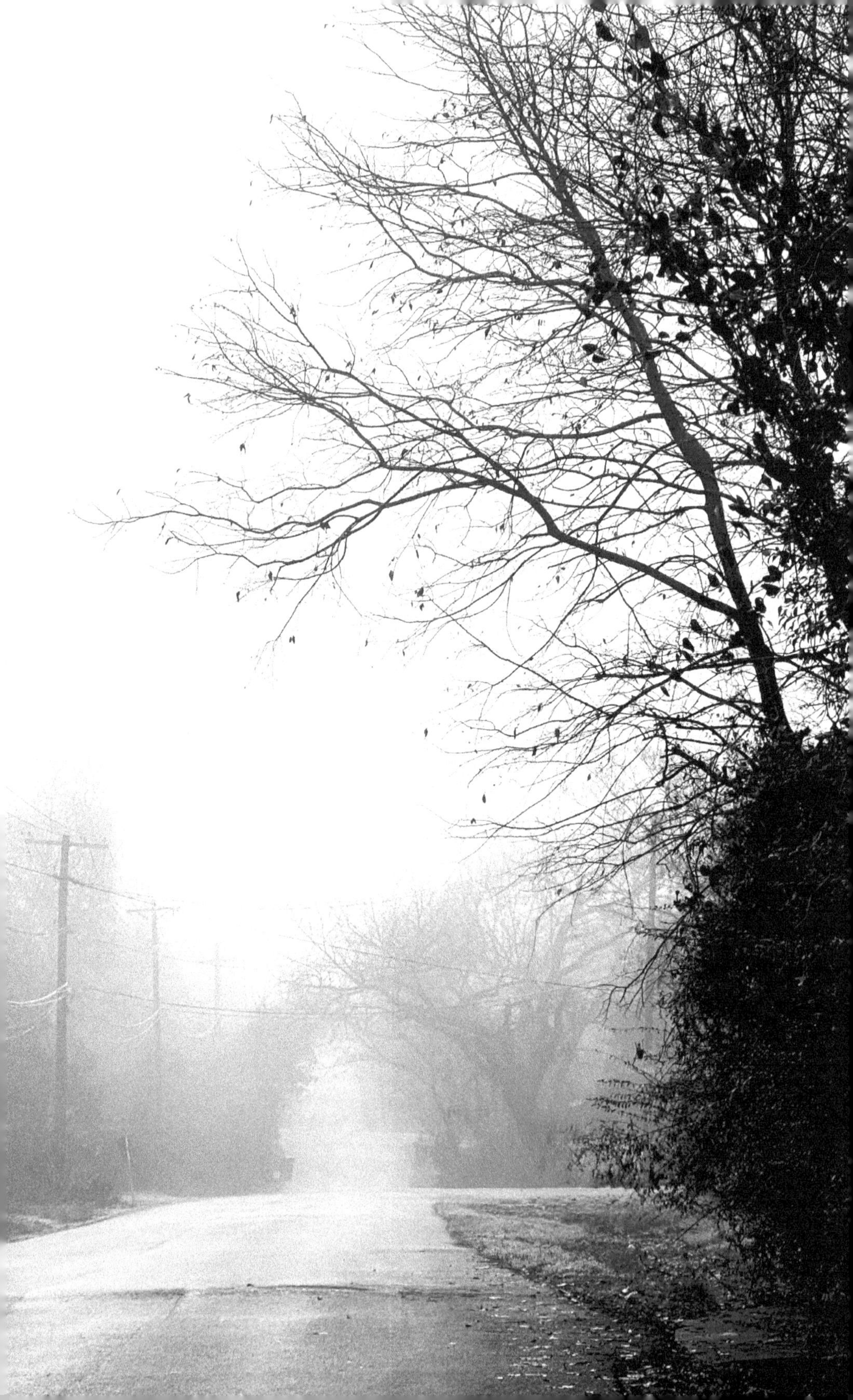

HERE

Okay, I am here. And if I am here, then I am not at home, not in my PJs, and not sitting by the fire. Honestly, I'd rather be home, still in my jammies at eleven in the morning, almost afternoon; still drinking coffee and still distracted by all my home beckons me to do . . . not that I would do any of it anyway. On days like today, I am really good at doing nothing. Instead, I am here, at my favorite coffee shop with mismatched tables and not one identical chair in the place.

I came here to write, and in doing so, to practice stepping out of my comfort zone, my sweet spot. To metaphorically and physically move. Admittedly, *here* is not much of a leap from *there.* It's more like a big step, and it is fairly comfy in a "not at home" kinda way. *Here* is a damn cool place with a warm vibe, even on a cold and dreary day. Today, I dressed in layers, topped off by a sweater that is just a bit too warm. If I try to take the sweater off, I'll make a spectacle of myself; much like a *Three Stooges* episode where they get all tangled up in their clothes, spinning, twirling, somersaulting, slapping each other, and, of course, getting poked in the eyes just to get out of their clothes. God help me if I slap one of my neighbors in an effort to get out of my sweater. So here I am on a cold and dreary, gray, winter day, sweating.

The melancholy indie tunes wafting overhead belie the hum of multiple and simultaneous conversations, the whir of modern appliances, and the buzz of people at work. And if you are not careful, you will catch a caffeine buzz just from the smell alone. Here, in addition to their regular duties, people are working on an upcoming charity event happening tomorrow, so the buzz is elevated to that of a busy beehive. Sometimes there and here don't have to be very different, but moving from here to there can simply change the narrative, even if it is all in my head. Most of the time, the *here* doesn't matter. Neither does *there*. Just changing directions can change the way I feel or think and get me going in a more positive direction. In the eighties, presidents Ronald Reagan and Mikhail Gorbachev came to an impasse during treaty negotiations while at Camp David. President Reagan then suggested they take a walk.

This simple action of literally and metaphorically moving forward got the conversations flowing again, and an agreement soon followed. For now, though, it is time to find a different *here* because at this moment, *here* now matters. The personality just shifted from funky coffee shop, bohemian-artsy workspace to a millennial-mothers-time-out-with-toddlers given free rein of *here,* and that includes my space. And just like that, the narrative changes . . . again. I'm not in the mood for toddlers talking in the only volume they know—loud and louder. Neither am I in the mood for the millennial mothers goo-goo'ing and ga-ga'ing over their free-reigning, space-invading babies. But such is the nature of any given narrative, colored by the environment. It changes, and either I change it, change with it, or it changes me.

HOW WAS THE FUNERAL?

Mom came home from the funeral dressed in obligatory black, looking a bit lost, with her eyes red and swollen from crying. Dad stayed home to babysit us while she went to the funeral for one of her cousins. Now home, she finds her seat at our kitchen table; the table where our family life happens. We gather as a family here and eat meals here. We play games here, and we have serious "talks" here. There are one to two boards that are added to the table to make it longer, thereby making it possible to include more people, more family, more games, and more talks.

The table is simple and kind of Amish in its uncomplicated, utilitarian appearance. At each of our places there are areas where the varnish is all but worn off, leaving spots of nearly naked wood. Those are the spots we place our hands and, much to my mother's constant consternation, our elbows. My sister and I often do our homework at the table, so there are letters and words and numbers etched into the wood from heavy-handed writing as we solve math problems and write out all kinds of answers to all kinds of homework questions. Over the years, it has come to look more like code than anything imaginably decipherable. As Mom slumped in sadness in her chair, Dad asks, "How was the funeral?" At this point, I am old enough to know what a funeral is and think this a weird question. In my mind, there is no other answer than, "It was horrible."

Yesterday, I went to the funeral of a good friend, and it wasn't horrible. A friend of eighteen years passed, and in our heyday, we were close. We were not so close when she died, so her passing has me thinking about all kinds of things, mostly friends and friendship. I listen to the rewind and replay of her life by her preacher, and it is sort of like listening to stories around a campfire. It is sweet and funny, nostalgic, and at times sad. The stories and mood leave me oddly hoping this evening will never end. Much like the end of the night after being around the campfire when everyone sings, "Mmm, I want to linger, mmm, a little longer, mmm, a little longer with you…" And I do! I want to linger a little bit longer in the memories of my friend.

In the South, especially in the South, anyone with knowledge of the Bible can hang a shingle on a building and call it a church. The preacher of the little church on Garland Road heard the knock of God's calling and hung his shingle. He made the place into a watering hole for your soul. The congregation is small and comprised of misfits. There are homeless, near homeless, LBGTQ, and other cultural unwanteds wandering the margins of society. Their collective heart is far bigger and collective pockets far deeper than any Stepford megachurch known to populate the South. My friend found a home here, and they loved her for nothing but her odd and peculiar self. She found a life here, and today, they celebrated that life. This is a church I would want to call home—and who knows, maybe I will. Metaphorically, it felt like sitting at the family kitchen table again.

The air conditioner quit working earlier in the day at the little church on Garland Road. Even the sundown service is no match for the remaining scorcher of a summer that smolders into the early fall of Texas. The calendar, at least, says it is early fall. The heat says IT'S STILL SUMMER, SUCKAS! We sit among friends, and we sit among strangers. We are sweating and fanning ourselves all the while remembering our friend and praising God in good ole fashion, Southern exuberance and Southern style, which, by the way, is now second nature to this Catholic transplant. By the end of the night, we are all fast friends. . . minus one.

I learned things about my friend I did not know. I did know she was generous beyond the comprehension of most bank accounts and most do-gooders, but her generosity went way beyond even my understanding. I did not know she was pretty sick her last few months, either.

Friendship is not always convenient or easy, and it is not measured in likes, favors, or reciprocity. Personally, I think favors and reciprocities are traps. I think friendship is measured in mistakes and do-overs and forgiveness. Friendship is beautifully sloppy and imperfectly messy. It's incongruous, inconvenient, and inconcise. It ebbs and flows, burns hot and fast; it smolders and sometimes burns out. Friendship, like fire, can hurt, and like yanking a hand back after getting burned on a hot stove, we pull our emotions back a bit, learning to be more cautious. Also as with fire, friendship keeps me feeling warm and safe. It's the battleground of forgiveness and the playground for love. There are too many variables in lives, personalities, and people to pigeonhole how friendship occurs. Like oxygen to a fire, the basic ingredient and fuel to friendship is love.

There are many friends I wish could have stayed until we grew old together. There are some I have lost along the way and

Friendship is not always convenient or easy and it is not measured in likes, favors or reciprocity. It is measured in mistakes and do-overs and forgiveness.

are forever that age when we lost track of each other. There are others who have hurt me beyond the boundaries of a mortal heart (it happened when I was thirteen), and now that I am fifty, it all seems so silly and not worth the punishment of being banished to "the island of misfit friends." There are so many people that fill the periphery of my circle of friends. I am close with some, and we have an unspoken agreement: "Love is all there is." Translation: we may not talk much, and we may see each other even less, but our love remains unwaveringly strong and always on alert! There are many scenarios, people, possibilities, and much variability; as long as love and common sense are present, I think we will all be okay!

Her funeral leaves me sad we lost touch. Her memorial reminds me it really is okay. I left the little church on Garland Road loving and hugging a little bit more the friends I do have. At the end of the evening, it felt like we were all sitting at the proverbial kitchen table where family and friends gather, and all manner of life occurs.

IF LIFE IS A BOWL OF CHERRIES, MAKE LEMONADE

Have you ever had one of those days where the only person that gets you is your nearly blind and half-deaf dog with dementia? My sweet dog gets lost when she finds herself on the other side of the bed. This is my day today. And to make matters worse, everything is fine. Work is going well, money in the bank, food in the fridge, wife is happy, and I haven't pissed off anyone, at least that I know of, anyway. And yet, while everything is humming along and totally in tune, I feel out of sync with all of it. Out of balance, off key, drawing the short straw, and flying headlong against near hurricane-strength winds. So in the urban jungle I call home, I go to my contemplative space, my balcony. It's four stories up and looks over the lights and sounds and activity of the city. In the morning, I get the sunrise, and in the waning light of the day, I see the city's flickering lights emerge. Today happens to be gray and dreary, a perfect backdrop to my mood. Earlier this morning, I even blamed the grayness for my mood.

I stand on my fourth-floor balcony and contemplate running away. Maybe I'll go see my sister and the kids. My niece and nephew are teenagers now. Teenage angst always makes me feel better about my own. And teenage drama makes mine pale in comparison, even though I now know my drama is completely fabricated by hyperthyroid demons that have taken up residence in the deep recesses of my psyche. Like squatters, they have secretly domiciled themselves without my permission and certainly without my blessing. Being tenants for many years, they are comfortable and refuse to move. Most of the time, I am able to corral them, but from time to time, their pestilence escapes my diligence and invades, then occupies my thoughts. I have taken courses, read books, meditated (and medicated), and listened to podcasts to exorcise them. Yet they persist and get uglier. All this due diligence seems to fuel them, kinda like throwing high voltage at Magneto in the *X-Men*. It did not slow him down a bit; it made him stronger.

One of my mom's favorite books was *If Life Is a Bowl of Cherries, Why Am I in the Pits?* by Erma Bombeck. She also tried to live by the expression, "If life hands you lemons, make lemonade." In this topsy-turvy mood of mine, I can't make lemonade or deal with the pits. This morning, I feel like a stranger in a very normal place, an utterly, completely normal place where there are no pits to define my mood and no lemonade to be made to shift my mood. And perhaps, in this place of mundane normalcy, is somewhere to be grateful. And maybe, just maybe, I will get lemonade from a bowl of cherries.

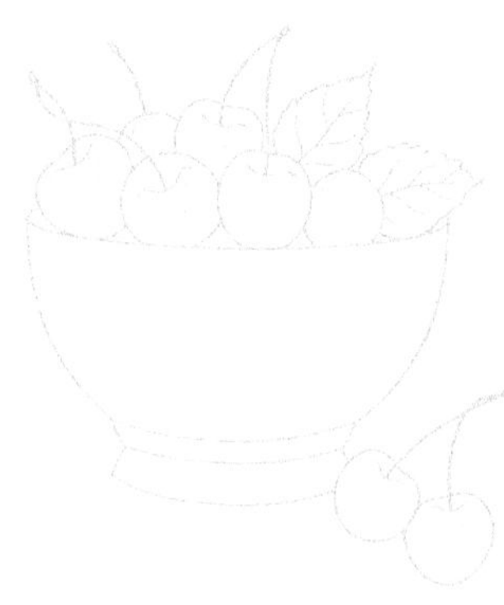

 FUMBLES, STUMBLES, AND GRUMBLES

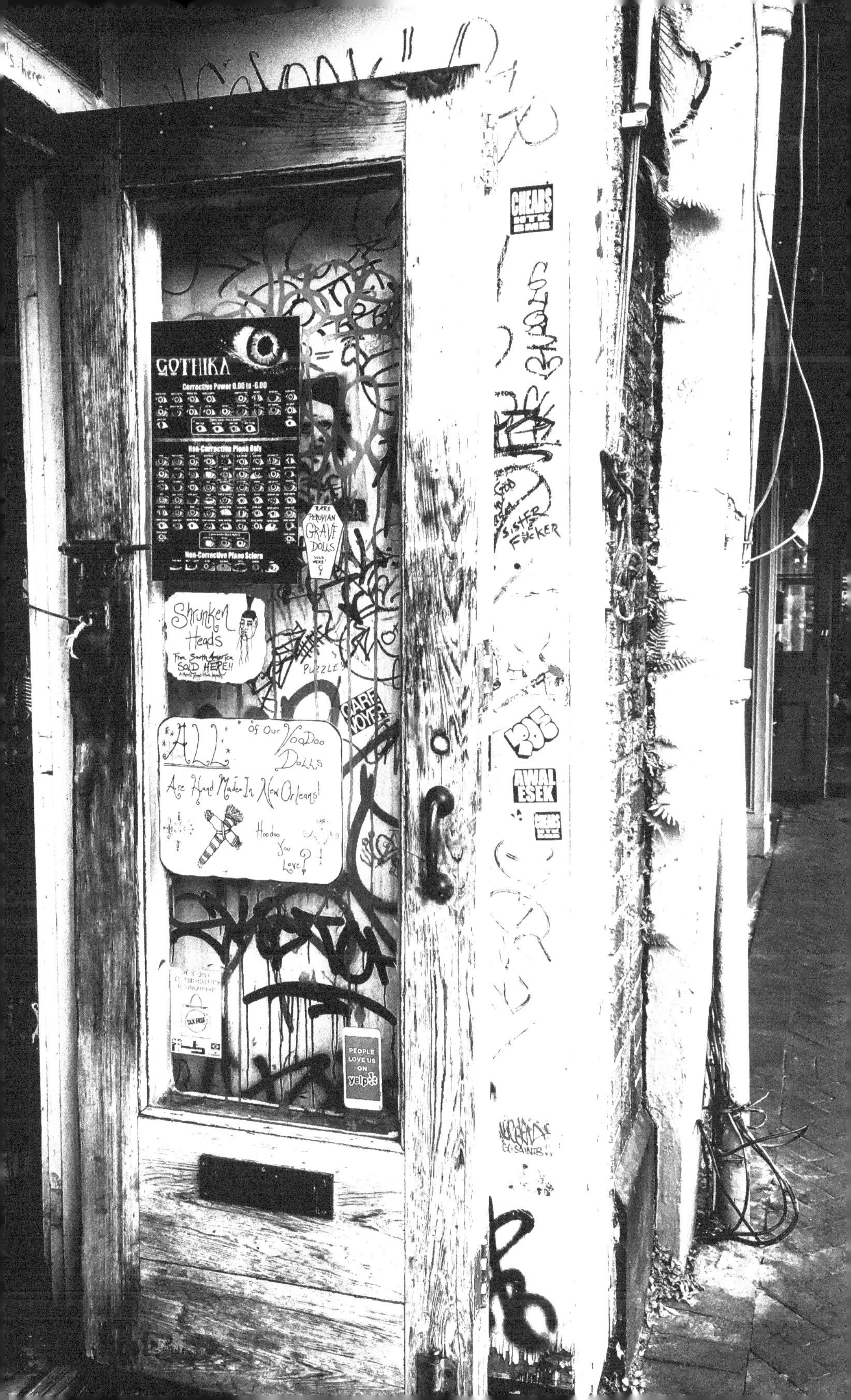
GOTHIKA
Corrective Power 0.00 to -6.00
Non-Corrective Plano Only
Non-Corrective Plano Sclera
RARE
PERUVIAN
GRAVE
DOLLS
SOLD
HERE!
Shrunken
Heads
From South America
SOLD HERE!!
PUZZLES
CARE
VOYE
ALL of Our VooDoo
Dolls
Are Hand Made In New Orleans!
Hoodoo
You
Love?
TAX FREE
PEOPLE
LOVE US
ON
yelp
CHEARS
MTK
BMB
GOD
SISTER
FUCKER
1985
AWAL
ESEK
CHEARS
BMB
GO SAINTS!!

THE SPACE BETWEEN

The distance between light and dark

Is a worn and crooked line

Where mourners follow a shrouded patriarch

The voices of sirens are unfettered and bold;

Light is imprisoned in a timid heart

And love lives between the shadows and cold.

Reflections of a once and forgotten life

From the depths tease a precious memory

Now nothing but dust recalls Lott's wife.

The space between black and white;

Where calm belies a dangerous current

And a furied torment does ignite.

FOUND

I looked under rocks,
Looked to the stars
And into the depths of oceans
I listened to water
As it trickled over river rocks
And crashed onto sandy shores
I listened to the wind
Rush across the plains
And whip through trees
I saw beauty and emptiness
Staring back at me with nothing
But the sounds of silence
Then I found you
Then I found me

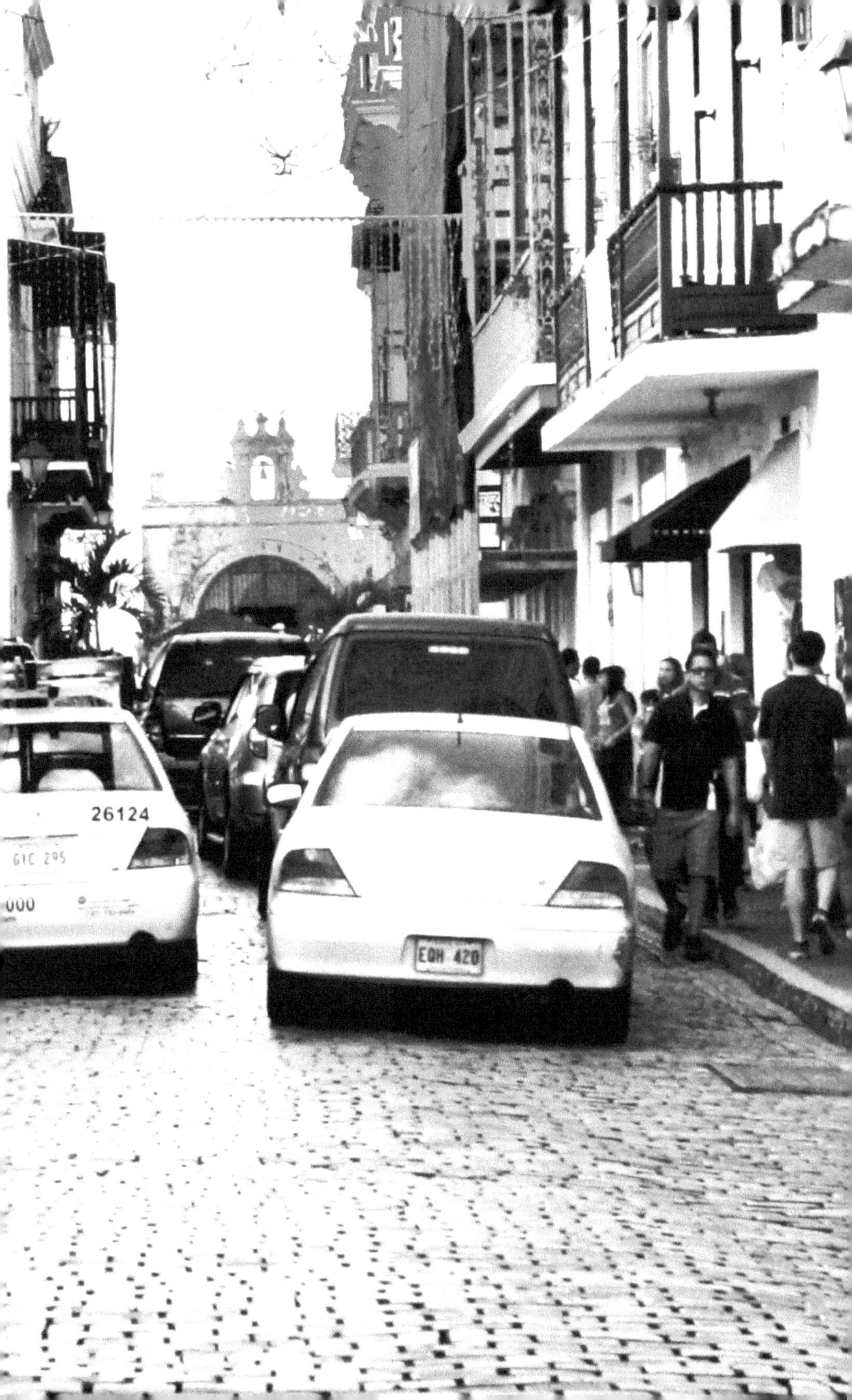

IT WAS A
LONG TIME AGO

Two of the greatest myths perpetuated on humanity are "It was a long time ago" and "It seems like just yesterday." Do you remember your first love? Depending on how it all went down, it might be your second or third. But I remember! And *it was a long time ago* and *it seems like just yesterday.* My mom died twenty years ago, and yes, *it was a long time ago,* and yep, *it seems like just yesterday.* Some days I feel like I am going through her illness and death all over again. Scars are like the still waters of the deep variety. Rip, peel, or wash off the scab, and the bleeding begins again. Every. Single. Time. It is always there, the deep wound just below the surface.

Remember the kid that bullied you? Or maybe you were that kid, and now you are a very different person. *It was a long time ago but seems like just yesterday,* doesn't it? When I think about that kid who bullied me, my heart races, and I am instantly transported back some thirty-plus years. I relive those events like they were just yesterday, but really, it was a long time ago. Ask me about it some day, and I will tell you the story over a beer or coffee, your choice; there is a plot twist and the good guy really does win.

I remember fondly and sweetly one of my first loves. I wasn't old enough to drink, but I was old enough to get my heart broken. That, at least, seems like it should be reserved for adults only, just as much as the alcohol. *It was a long time ago AND it seems like just yesterday.* As much as those memories tug at my heart, so does my current and last love. We got together ten years ago and, you got it, *it was a long time ago.* And *it really does seem like just yesterday.* As far as some of my most cherished memories go, this one is new. The point is, it was a long time ago and it seems like just yesterday! It really is a kind of mind f*&k, isn't it?

A long time ago and just yesterday go hand in hand like good cop bad cop, peanut butter and jelly, and wasabi peas (only because I bought some today-yum!). One certainly can exist without the other, but together the team is more effective. The idea, *seems like yesterday*, keeps the memories fresh, vivid. We just have to go back to the last place we sat, or the last room we were in to find whatever we lost. *It was a long time ago* keeps the memories tucked away in the recesses and corners of our memory. And to retrieve them is like going into the attic and blowing the dust off the old trunk before you open it to sort through what's inside.

I say, "Yes" to both. Yes, to peanut butter and jelly, yes to wasabi peas, yes to it was a long time ago, and yes to it seems like yesterday!

With both we wax nostalgic

STEP THROUGH

Today there seems to be a pervasive mood to the world and in our goings-on. We flipped the pages of the calendar until finally, a new year emerged, and with each turn we hoped things would get closer to normal. As the months disappeared, the struggles of 2020 did not. Even as the days begin to get longer and brighter, the corners are still dark. Our uncertainty lingers as a flood of collective grief lays in wait underneath thinly veiled anger. And worse, there is a complacency that has blanketed the planet, numbing us into an unwanted, though emerging, reality.

Our lives have been upended, and in grasping for security, some of us locked the doors, barred the windows, or closed our hearts. Some of us did all of it. With the restrictions on human contact and connection, the absence of something as simple as a hug has never been so loudly heard or so painfully missed.

In this darkness, we forget there is a light. We forget we hold that light, and that light is creative. So get creative! Begin to wonder, *How?* How do I get that promotion? How do I keep my family happy? How do I get a job when it seems like there are none? How do I keep from going crazy during a lockdown? The answer may not be there right away, but just wondering will put you on a path you didn't even know and open doors you didn't know existed. Remember, not all doors are rectangular with a knob. Some are hatches, portholes, rabbit holes, even secret passages with a secret code. Draw an imaginary door in the air and step through. The act of stepping through puts your body in motion and sends the universe a message.

Kindness is the conduit through which that creative energy flows. It pours into the hearts of the suffering, eases the pain of the hurting, sheds a glimmer of hope into the hearts of the broken, and flickers in the darkest corners. It has no boundaries. It is not constrained by our circumstances. It is the energy of love—and with love, all things are possible. So find your door, even if you have to create your own.

And step through. . . .

 FUMBLES, STUMBLES, AND GRUMBLES

I LOVE...

I love the sound of bare feet on a tile floor,

the chill of fall that has me hunger for more

I love the feel of grass between my toes,

the smell of jasmine as it catches my nose

I love to see sheets hung to dry, fluttering in the breeze,

the taste of a campfire on my lips, reaching for the trees

I love the shade on a hot day and the sun on a winter window sill

I love a long road trip and sitting still

I love. . . .

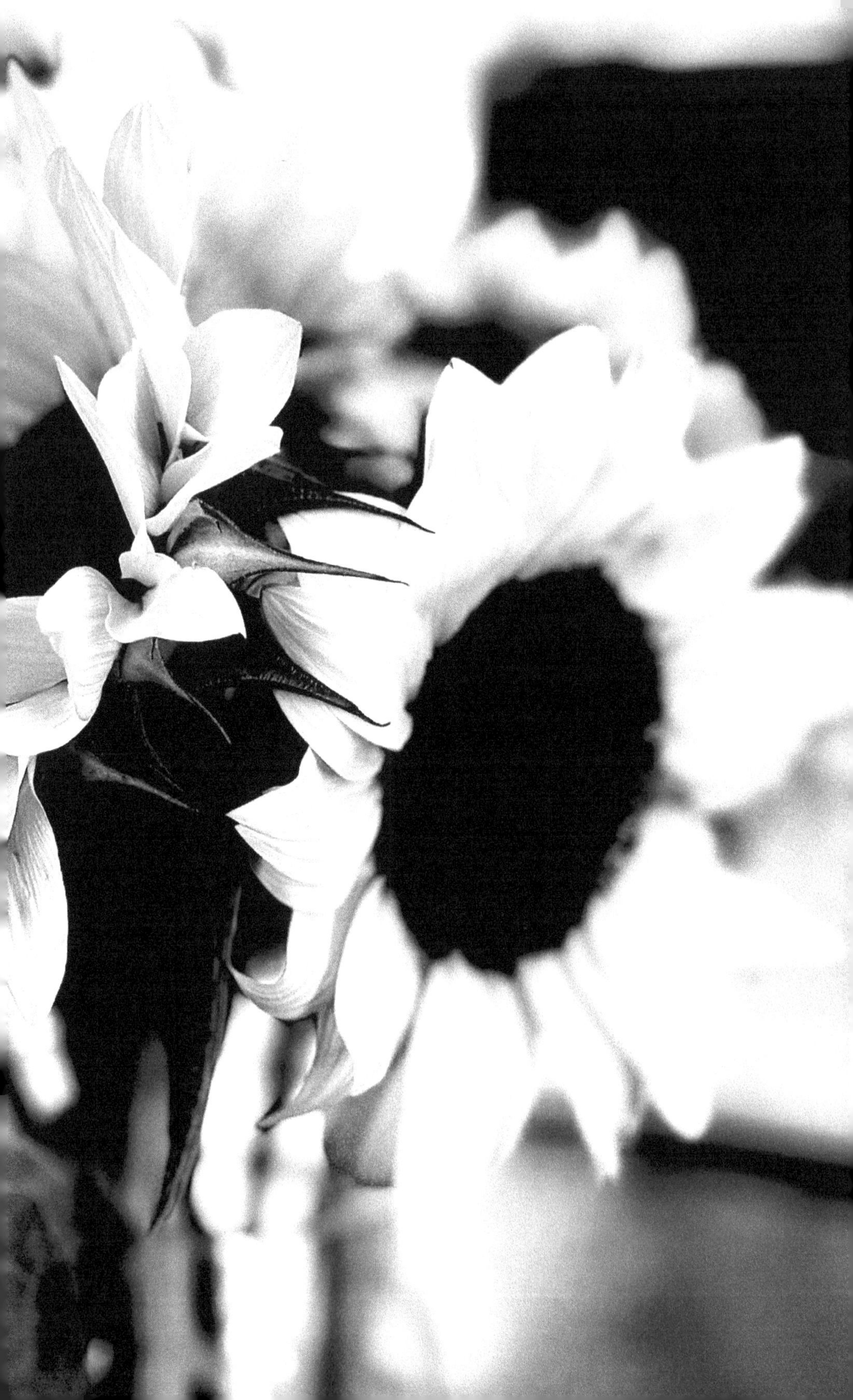

NOWHERE ON EARTH

The phrase "nowhere on earth" is often used to convey enormity and complexity. When something is missing despite exhaustive efforts, one might say, "It is nowhere on earth." We are given a sense of the effort made in looking, a sense of complete and utter futility at a fruitless search, and a sense of the exhausting endeavor to find what is lost. Weary searchers would then proclaim, "It's nowhere on earth!" I dare say this expression comes from a sense that there is nothing beyond Earth, a planetary-centric point of view, if you will.

Today we are traveling more than ever before and reaching corners of the globe once only known to explorers and intrepid adventurers. Indeed, the world is becoming a much smaller place, made even smaller by the far-reaching and never-sleeping tentacles of the internet and social media. Maybe one day, when someone proclaims, "It's nowhere on earth," I will be left with hope. Hope, like having to search just the bedroom and living room for my glasses, as opposed to having to retrace a whole day's worth of steps. After searching one room, we move on to the next. After searching one planet, we move on to the next, and perhaps it really could be as easy as moving on to the next room.

As I was watching one of the many iterations of *Star Trek*, the Captain was pondering the origins of a phone call. Well, I say phone call. I think he called it a transmission. He discovered it was an "off-world" call. He pondered out loud, saying, "It came from nowhere on earth." When said like that, it was no big deal. It was more a statement of fact.

Years ago, to get or make a long-distance call *was* a big deal. It was costly, reception was often bad, and in the early days, you had to get an operator to connect a long-distance call for you. Cell phones have made that obsolete. No one really noticed when long-distance calls went away. They were just absorbed into our daily life of cell phone use. Now it is just as easy to call India as it is Indiana. And no one noticed. We call home, whether it is Mexico, Ireland, India, or China just as easily as we call our bestie for drinks. While calls come from anywhere on earth, my glasses are often, still, *nowhere on earth.*

MENDED

The strongest heart is one that's mended with the threads of experience, years of hurts and regrets. Those mended pieces were once bits of misconceptions and non-truths that could not bear the pull of a true calling. It gave way to the weight of what does not belong in my heart. That mended heart, that patchwork heart, is the canvas of life. Each mended rip, each tear, each patched-up hole, and each repaired, shattered piece is a memory, a fragment of the whole, the whole of me.

Today we have the ability to repair things and make them better, stronger than the original. The same is true of our emotions. We know more about our inner workings than ever before and have the technology to become much stronger for it.

I wear that heart proudly and show off the scars. The loose strings and tattered edges ripple in the winds of life. I tell myself, *do not be afraid*. Be brave and peek under the raised edges. It's a Band-Aid, and it's ready to come off. Grit your teeth and let 'er rip—whether it's the secret that gets out and becomes a lesson in discernment, the unanswered prayer that becomes the open door through which walked my one true love, the heartbreak that taught me independence, and the knowing of utterly, completely, undeniably, how strong I am. This is me; this is us. We all have scars. You know, you got this. It is the canvas of life. It is all that has made you or broken you. There are no do-overs, so what do you say? I say, "YES."

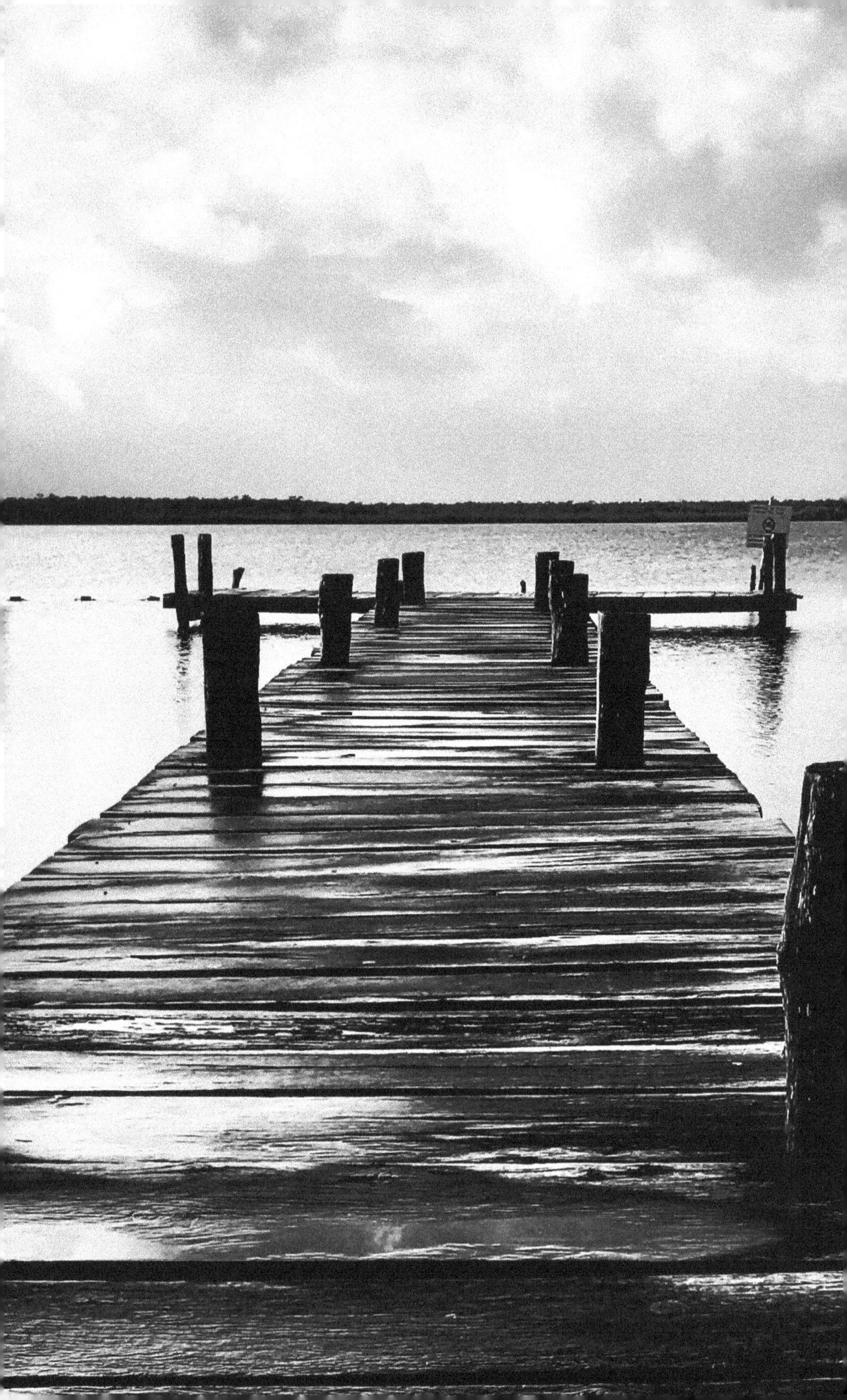

WATER OFF
A DUCK'S BACK

I am a brooder, and brooders brood. Before there was resting bitch face, there was me trying to explain the expression I make when lost in thought. I still prefer brooding to resting bitch face, no matter how culturally *apropos*.

I once tried to tell a friend I was easygoing about life and further explained that things just rolled off me like water off a duck's back. She about fell over laughing because this was the furthest from the truth. At that time, I was not aware of my brooding tendencies, the sullenness of being lost in thought. I was also not aware that I tended to be serious, sober, and mullish.

Since then, it has been a goal to live the way of water rolling off a duck's back. Fighting all the possible battles, real or crafted by my sense of what's fair, is exhausting. Living in that perpetual state of battle does damage to me physically and mentally. It became the filter through which all my memories passed and by which my present life is colored.

So in the world of clichés, I adopted and adapted these three: 1) Pick your battles, 2) The water you swim in, and 3) Fake it 'till you make it. This became my blueprint for living a life that rolled, like water, off a duck's back.

I actively work on maintaining my peace in traffic and with stupid people because that is a given here in Dallas. I am surrounded by both. Choosing to live in Dallas is choosing to live with traffic and a variety pack of stupid. Picking a fight with either is a fruitless endeavor, and so, in picking my battles, I choose not to fight these as well as many, many, oh so many others.

I work at a rather large county hospital, and we deal with all that humanity has to offer, including all the nastiness people can dish out. Nonetheless, I love my job and keep going back because I choose the ugliness and the beauty that comes along with it. Getting my feelings hurt by the names or insults lobbed at me is like tilting at windmills. Getting frustrated with our time-off system or clocking-in-and-out system is also a fruitless endeavor. It is the water I swim in, and it became my choice when I signed the contract eleven years ago.

There are those moments when all my complaints are let loose upon the world. I wail in frustration that the traffic is a cruel and unusual punishment set upon the unsuspecting citizenry or the time-off system isn't fair, and I was tricked into accepting this detail as if my contract had line-item privileges. It's these moments where I have to take a deep breath, count to ten, and deal with my feelings. I put on my bullshit-wearing boots. The ones that come up to my knees because I am about to wade into the mire of the world just turning on its axis and paying me no mind. With my proverbial BS boots on and a forced smile on my face, I step gingerly and fake it 'till I make it.

Eventually, I am able to swing back to center and proceed through my day, picking my battles like a toddler picking her nose, boldly, out in the open, and unashamed. In moments of clarity, I'll grab a float and a margarita to navigate those waters in which I'd normally be dog-paddling or worse, swimming upstream.

And through it all, I will brood because brooders brood. This monologue is a product of brooding. Most of the time now, the waters of life do roll off my back and sometimes things stick to me like mud on a duck. Eventually though, it all gets shaken off.

LISA MARIE

My junior and senior years were spent in a small Catholic boarding school. I was thrilled to escape the bullying that had followed me like a dark cloud from Milwaukee all the way to Dallas. The mean girl antics here were more subtle and less scarring than the vicious public-school variety I had endured. There were a handful of fellow misfits at Woodlands Academy Of The Sacred Heart, who made me feel somewhat at home—about as at home as a long-lost cousin crashing the family reunion for a seemingly endless weekend.

When I arrived at that holy prison, I left behind my very first girlfriend. I tried to keep my lesbian tendencies on the downlow, but never really put much effort into hiding it. Kids will be kids—they judged this book by its cover, and eventually the snide remarks, snickers, and finger-pointing started. It was still a reprieve from the hell of Dallas though. Those ruler-wielding penguins had powers far beyond those of regular teachers! Their ability to silence the most vicious verbal assaults with a mere glance and the dull jingle of rosary beads was magical.

Lisa and I—can I use your real name?—became besties, and to this day she swears I was her rock. I had absolutely no clue back then, though…none whatsoever. I was simply trying to keep my own demons from devouring me whole.

Mercifully, my demons seemed to corral hers. Anytime her

"fun" demons started to push her into the danger zone, my "worry" demons would rein her in, keeping her safe from any real harm. We were quite the pair, my trouble-making bestie and I. Our days were filled with jokes, laughter, and mischief.

Always running fashionably late, Lisa would barrel into the school parking lot, tires screeching and the driver's window cracked while billowing smoke signals danced from the end of her cigarette. I'd hop in her land yacht of a car—a massive Buick that qualified as its own maritime vessel—and we'd impart on after-school adventures and weekend escapes.

We'd spend hours chatting it up as we sailed over road craters and speed bumps, deftly navigating the suburban Chicago streets like a hot knife gliding through butter. With one hand on the wheel, and the other one flicking a cigarette, Lisa swore her parents were oblivious to her questionable and toxic habit. Who knows? Maybe they were. I'm still baffled...

Spring brought volleyball followed by softball; fall ushered in Halloween; and winter gifted us with Christmas shenanigans, where we'd drive all over creation just to gaze in wonder at the kaleidoscope of lights. This is still one of my most favorite things to do.

In a rare role reversal, I taught Lisa the sacred art of driving a stick shift, now known as a Millennial anti-theft device. My sister, Kim, and I, shared a white Plymouth Horizon—basically, America's sad attempt at recreating the VW Rabbit's magic, stick shift and all.

We piled in the tragically unhip Horizon and headed to the airport during Christmas break. The plan was to have Lisa ride with us, drop us off, and then take the car back to her place for the two weeks we'd be gone for vacation.

We pulled up to the airport, climbed out of the car, and I tossed her the keys.

"Wait! I don't know how to drive a fu**ing stick!" she yelped, her voice spiking an octave or two as the panic set in.

"You'll figure it out," I assured her, confident in her abilities.

And figure it out she did!

Lisa was a pro by the time she picked us up at the airport two weeks later. Although, she admitted to doing her fair share of bucking, lurching, and stalling during that inadvertent vision quest back to the 'burbs.

I eventually spilled the big secret to her—that I batted for the other team, if you catch my drift. This revelation sent her scrambling down the hall to the chapel in a traumatized frenzy. Lisa wasn't really the praying sort; it was just the only empty room she could find. Our homeroom teacher, Sister Finn, caught her mid-meltdown, and they had a little heart-to-heart. Once Lisa rejoined the land of the undisturbed, she found me where she ditched me, her dramatic Italian tendencies on full display.

Mercifully my demons seemed to coral hers. Anytime her "fun" demons started to push her into the danger zone, my "worry" demons would rein her in.

"Sooo…are you attracted to me?" she asked, equal parts curious and cautious.

I cocked my head and arched a pointed brow at her. "Uh, no," was my response.

"What? Why not? I'm cute!" she counterclaimed, feigning indignation.

And so began my endless quest to explain that being gay didn't mean being attracted to every girl, just like straight girls aren't into every guy they encounter. Go figure.

Our friendship continued to thrive through graduation, right up until the day I left Chicago in my rearview mirror, without looking back, and without so much as a goodbye. I figured no one would miss me, so I slipped away, never looking back.

Years of emotional turmoil taught me not to get too attached to others. After all, friends disappoint you, people leave, and I simply didn't have the heart to cope with that kind of ache.

Fast forward thirty-five years, and who should come knocking on my virtual door but Lisa herself, courtesy of Facebook's all-seeing eye. I'm pretty sure I ugly cried for a solid two weeks straight. It wasn't until that moment I realized just how much I had missed her, and how much I had missed out on by inadvertently cutting ties.

When she asked why I never reached out, I confessed that I genuinely believed she wouldn't even notice my absence.

Her response?

A loving, exasperated "Dumbass."

She's been calling me dumbass ever since.

Love you, Lisa.

WHAT'S YOUR NAME, CHILD?

What's your name, child?
What does your mama call you?
What does your daddy say about you?
What's your name, child?
On the day you were born, the stars aligned.
And sent you in a direction as obliged.
What's your name, child?
The winds whispered a tale of deeds to be done;
The trees rustled in baited anticipation.
What's your name, child?
Do you know the strength of your light?
The dark corners you are destined to ignite?
What's your name, child?
Your heart is ordained; filled with love and tenacity
Your journey is consecrated and demanding ferocity.
What's your name, child….?

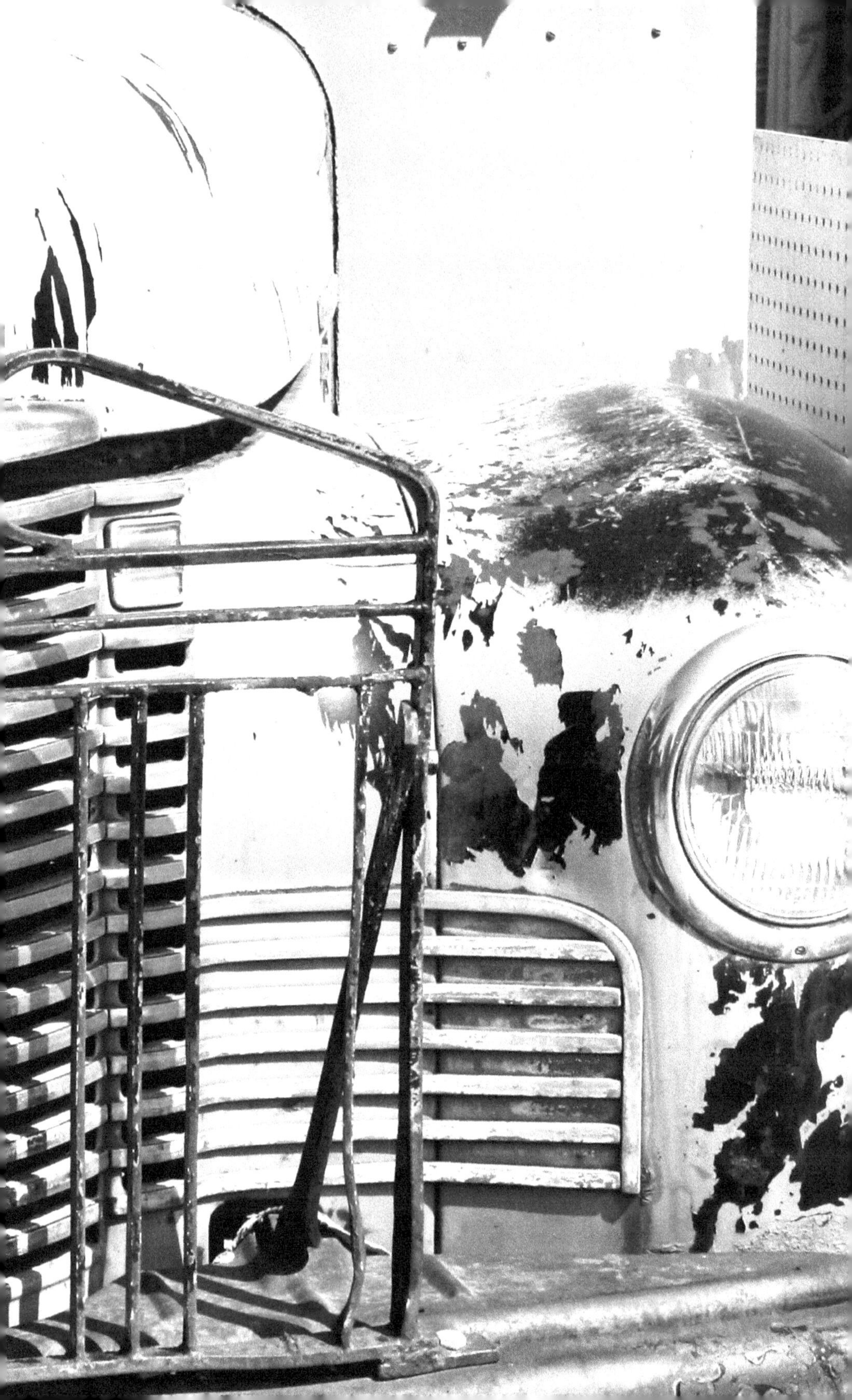

METAPHORICAL ME

Nowadays, social media is flooded with well-meaning advice and positive sayings on how to live your best life. Phrases like, "*Be like a tree and let the dead leaves drop,*" or "*The wind does not break a tree that bends,*" rain down in front of us as we scroll through our feeds. Spiritual and transformational leaders pour out thought-provoking questions—like, "*Would you go for it if there was a million dollars at the end of this road?*"—all in an attempt to motivate us to work harder at our goals. And we can't forget the dog metaphors! My favorite is the one about aspiring to be as loyal and loving as my dog. I'm sure you've heard the one by John Grogan: "A dog does not care if you are rich or poor, educated or illiterate, clever or dull. Give them your heart, and they will give you theirs."

So here's the thing: I love the intention of all these metaphors, but guess what? I'm not a tree! Sure, I can bend, but I'd be lucky to bend enough to touch my knees at best! I know, I know, it's a metaphorical bend, but still, I am *not* a tree. In fact, metaphorically speaking, I have been known to bend too much, as in a pathological-people-pleasing kinda way.

As for letting dead leaves drop, that's hard for me, too. I suppose it's easier when it's a bad boss or an ass in traffic, but when it comes to long-time relationships, it is really hard for me to let go, especially of the toxic relationship that is my father.

And don't get me started on a million dollars? Really? You want to light a fire under me by pretending there's a million nonexistent dollars at the end of the road to achieving my goal? Like that pretend and nonexistent-existent money would be the reason I take a day off work, stay up late, or cancel plans with my family to chase my dreams? I'm probably going to chase them anyway, but not like that.

Yeah, in this vast pool of positivity, about the only metaphors that really give me "paws" are the ones about dogs. I used to have a lab/golden retriever mix that bounced out of bed in the morning, wagging her tail so fast her whole body wriggled. She would jump up and down while slobbering kisses on me to get me out of bed. To look at her was pure happiness. She loved everyone and would probably let in a potential burglar, smothering them with kisses as well. All she wanted in life was food, TLC, and to play ball. That's it.

I wish I could wake up like that—excited about the new day and the chance to do what I love all over again. I wish I could embrace humanity the way my dog loved people, slathering exfoliating kisses upon everyone and bouncing up to unsuspecting strangers. But unfortunately, there are some crappy people out there with whom I'd rather not associate, much less run up to them, wagging my metaphorical tail, and looking irresistibly "pet-me" cute!

Once, while visiting NYC, my wife and I got off at the wrong stop and unintentionally began following two random guys. After a short time of walking behind them in the same direction, they looked back at us and said, "Yeah, that's right, ladies, just follow us."

Nope! Nope! Nope! Not only no, but *HELL NO!* We did an abrupt about-face, got back on the train, returned to the hotel, called it quits for the night, and called room service. As much as I would like to not care if someone is smart, illiterate, rich or poor, what they drive, or what I drive, I do.

I have had a lifetime of trial and error to pick up bad (for lack of a better way to say it) habits. Having spent the better part of the last twenty years learning healthy habits and boundaries, I now feel like a toddler learning new ways of "being" while simultaneously trying to unlearn the old, pernicious behaviors.

Like a toddler, I fall a lot, throw tantrums, and don't want to get back up. I say I am trying to unlearn most of it because there were some good things that came out of the education that was my childhood. For one, I am quite empathetic, and now know that I cannot help or fix everyone, but damn, I'll still kill myself trying to rescue all the strays.

We are currently in the middle of a woke state, and there are all kinds of people claiming to be spiritually connected, living a transformed life. Those same people also come with all kinds of advice. Not all of it is good, though, and most appear to be one-size-fits-all.

However, life advice can never be one-size-fits-all, because each person's life has shaped them differently, and our shapes are in a constant state of change.

Over the years, I've tried on a variety of these universally sized practices and methodologies, desperate to find the thing that fits like a favorite sweater. What I got, however, is something more like a life jacket, complete with colorful patches of life experience that covered the holes that left me on the verge of drowning.

Yeah, yeah, yeah...I know. For someone who complains about metaphors, I sure am using a lot here. But that's ok. Because although I can't bend like a tree, don't have a million metaphorical dollars, and am far from slobbering the world with "paws-itivity," I'm learning that I can be the captain of my own ship, can weather any storm, and can feel confident knowing my life jacket of experience will keep the new and improved me afloat, even if I fall overboard.

DEATH

I saw him in the distance
Slowly coming closer
He looked familiar and foreign
He asked, do you know who I am?
I looked into his eyes.
What I saw scared and comforted me
He said, I am death.
Are you here for me?
No, said death, I am visiting
But you feel so close
I feel your chill; I feel your warmth
Embrace me and take me with
I'm not stopping for you, he said
Your time is on the horizon.
You can wait, though, not in life and not in death.

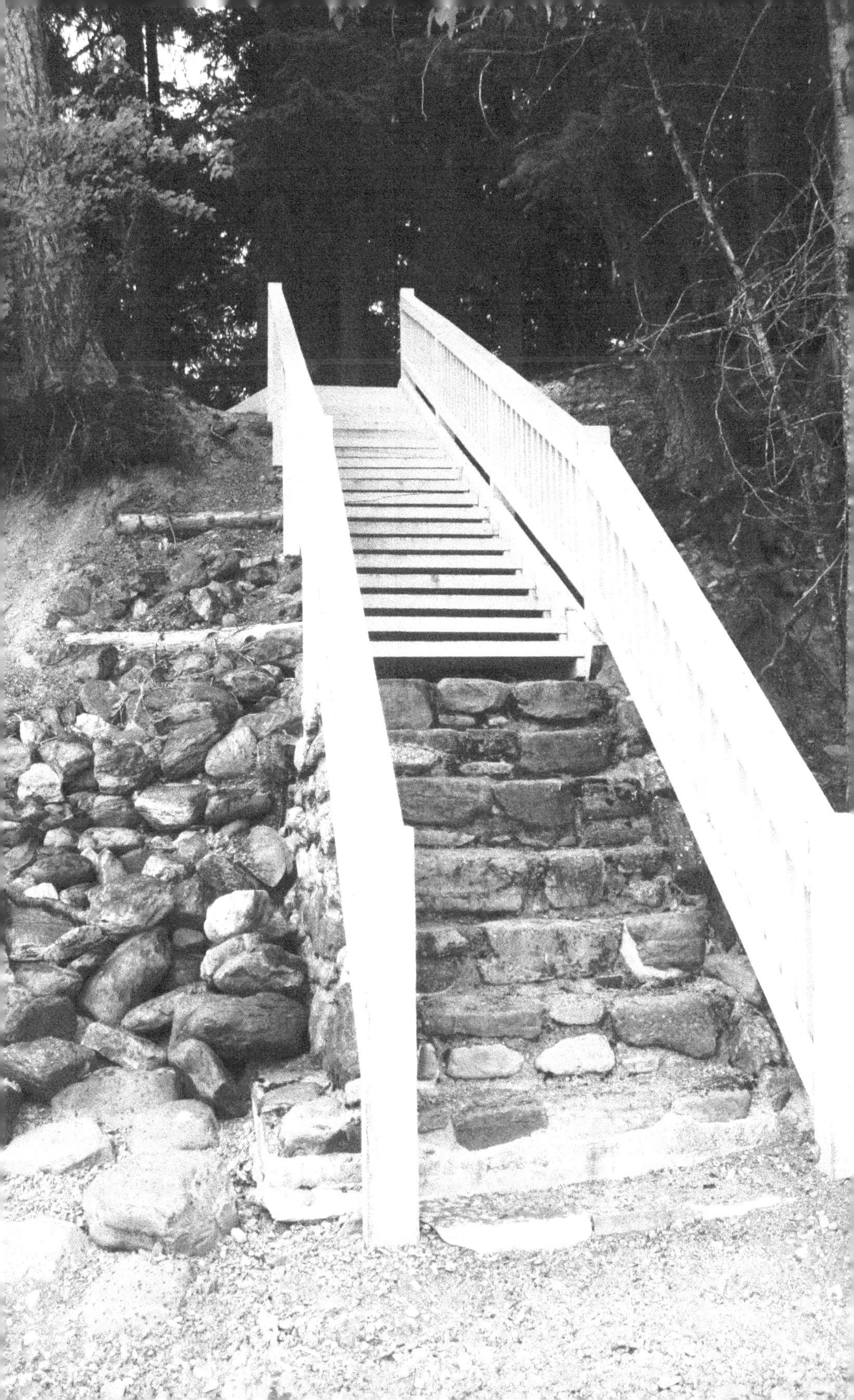

America's
Favorite
Tom Moore
10¢ CIGAR

A BUNNY RABBIT!

I turned down the street and made my way out of the neighborhood. Ours is a particularly busy street. There are lots of vehicles parked on our road—personal, recreational, and construction vehicles. The construction vehicles are the bane of my existence at the moment. They take over the street and the neighborhood, consuming pavement and space as if they were out in the vast Texas countryside instead of the ever-encroaching urban sprawl that is Dallas.

We live in a funky, artsy, blue-collar turned gentrified, bougie, neighborhood—a mishmash of bohemians, retirees, millionaires, and holdouts wanting to keep the houses small and the yards big. Not one cookie-cutter house is in sight, so you never know what display someone will have in front of their house. One home has a store mannequin dressed like a 1920's flapper, standing like an unblinking sentry through the seasons. In another yard is an almost life-size metal sculpture of a giraffe, painted with the requisite spots. We have a beekeeper with an ornate wildflower display, and a police officer with a manicured lawn below and a cats' playground of tubes and nets that wind in and out of their trees above.

Tomorrow was not only a regular trash day, but it was also a bulky trash pickup day, so all manner of refuse, recycling cans, debris, and garbage were out, lining the curbside to be picked up whenever the city got around to collecting it.

Having lost an hour of precious sleep (thanks to daylight-savings time kicking in during the early morning hours), I carefully drove down Eustis Avenue in the dark, navigating the minefield of parked cars, debris, and the occasional person walking their dog at 6:30 on a Sunday morning. This was normal for me, because Sunday was the first day of my work week. During the week, I duck and dodge all the neighbors leaving at the same time as I am, either on a caffeine buzz, three cups in, or zero cups in, rushing out in a semi-sleep stupor. This morning, though, despite all the curbside clutter, it was peaceful.

My high beams bounced around the clutter and chaos that is Monday mornings on the street I call home and to which I give my address. In the lights, my attention was caught by a small gray mess of fur darting left, then right, then left again in a frenzied moment of panicked indecisiveness. "A bunny! Oh, bunny, bunny, bunny!" my inner fiver-year-old squealed with joy.

It had been years since I'd last seen an old-fashioned gray rabbit with a fluffy tail. Seeing it literally filled my eyes with tears. The sheer simplicity of childlike joy from seeing a bunny in the dark quiet of the early morning was exquisite, and the emotion of it quite caught me off guard. I don't think I ever cried at seeing a rabbit before, but I did this morning!

When the five-year-old retreated and the adult re-emerged, I felt a tad foolish for crying at the sight of a little rabbit. In reality, however, I'd give anything to have more moments like that. More moments that fill me with uncomplicated, childlike joy. That feeling had me in such a place of pristine, pure happiness, that I wish I could experience it again and again in its purest form, every day, every hour, every minute.

Sometimes I get distracted by all the trash, clutter, and chaos lining my way that I miss the simple things—the bunnies of joy, so to speak—that hop in and out of my life. Maybe if I spend a little more time with my high beams on, I just might get my wish.

REPETITION

When working with people with traumatic brain injuries, repetition is essential. Repetition of movements, commands, words, and actions is vital until that thing becomes second nature again. Repetition also works well with young children. Donald Trump used repetition relentlessly, until people said the same thing as if they were chanting a mantra of sorts. "Lock her up" comes to mind almost immediately. Hitler did the same with the followers of his ideology, getting them to commit atrocious crimes. On a lighter note, so did Jesus and Buddha with words of light and encouragement.

Recently, I was listening to a book where the author was talking about terrorists who commit brutal and savage deeds with the promise of an afterlife, complete with seven virgins to ravage as they please as their reward. When I heard that, I didn't even flinch. That this exists is not the issue. That I didn't at least pause is.

Growing up, *Emergency* was one of my favorite shows. It was a drama centered around the lives of the firefighters and paramedics of Station 51 in Los Angeles. I caught an episode on cable the other day and started re-watching it, but couldn't finish. It was so slow compared to today's equivalent.

Over the years, TV and movies have gotten much faster and grittier just to keep our attention. We've become numb to the gore and disrespect of life. Today, mass shootings are so common that school children have to practice active shooter drills. We had to practice bomb drills growing up during the Cold War. At least then the enemy was another country, and our government spent millions to keep that enemy in check. Today's enemy is the kid next door, or maybe in the next seat, and so far, all we've gotten are thoughts and prayers from the government.

I feel like I'm part of one giant social experiment, perhaps called the repetition coefficient, where repetition of bad deeds is the coefficient, humanity is the variable, and the answer is our response. And because humanity is the variable, the answer will always change.

If math is the language of the universe and forty-two is the answer to everything, maybe I should look to a physicist for help. Or maybe I am thinking way too hard, and the answer really is too simple for a complicated mind.

Just for today, I don't need an answer. Just for today, I don't need an answer. Just for today, I don't need an answer…

SNOW DAYS

We grew up in Wisconsin. Say "Wisconsin" to most people, and they think cheese, Green Bay Packers, and snow—and not necessarily in that order.

It snows a lot in Wisconsin. It is a regular occurrence with a culture and all sorts of activities built around the snow. What didn't happen very often was "freezing rain" or "thunder snow." Yes, thunder snow! Another thing that didn't happen often was snow days.

The city rarely shut down due to snow, but if a hint of a rumor began to waft its way into whispers of school closings, all the school-aged children dreamt of snowmen, snow forts, and snowball fights! Our parents weren't afraid to drive in snow! No chains required! It is what we did. Snow days filled the dreams of each of us every winter, and on the rare occasion it happened, it was truly a gift from the snow gods.

Now, here in Texas, freezing rain and thunder snow are becoming regular events, like unwanted guests you can't get rid of, or the mother-in-law who overstays her welcome. Their arrival is a bold, flamboyant announcement to an unsuspecting audience. It becomes that obnoxious voice that carries above all the rest—the one you can't unhear, and the one you wish would just go away.

Say "snow day" in Texas, and everything stops, becoming paralyzed for a few days. It's not fair to compare Texas to Wisconsin.

To be honest, we don't really get snow days; we get ice days, and at some point, the snow we do get becomes the latter. Nobody can drive on ice, not even the most cold-hardy Wisconsinite among us!

Since moving to Texas, snow days have gone from the stuff of winter wonderland fairy tales, to a special kind of hell—the Texas hell that returns every June when we're desperately wishing for some frosty fun. No, not in the form of ice that fills our roads, but rather, ice for our margaritas! So shed that parka, and pass the salt!

NO MORE FIRSTS

I plopped into my favorite chair, grabbing the remote, and sitting all in one motion. I turned on the TV and caught the local news covering one of the doctors where I work. The news was high-lighting him as the first black doctor born in the Jim Crow South to be part of leading such a large institution. Specifically, he was born in a segregated ward of the hospital where he now occupies an executive suite.

I want to live in a world where there are no more firsts. No more "first female CEO of a Fortune 500 company," no more "first African-American leading a hospital department or major network news anchor," no more "first Latina with a Ph.D. in charge of a large school district," and where "woman-owned" or "black-owned" are not the leading reasons to support a business. Unfortunately, or fortunately, this kind of list can go on for infinity.

There has already been a first black president, but looking at the number of African-Americans in politics, the next one isn't going to be on the presidential podium anytime soon.

We have a history of unrecognized firsts with the likes of

Dorothy Vaughan, Mary Jackson, Katherine Johnson, and Christine Darden—NASA research mathematicians, also known as the "Hidden Figures."

Though the first African-Americans and first women to break through this particular glass ceiling, they were still treated as third-class citizens. And though this is mainstream information and the stuff of movies now, it took fifty-ish years to come to the forefront of our awareness.

Currently, the workforce of aerospace engineering at NASA is predominantly male and white. For those who care, here are the stats: 70.5% male, 72% white, 4% Hispanic or Latino, 10.8% Black or African-American, and 12% Asian. And this is just NASA.

I won't be celebrating until being a "first" is a matter of fact. At this time, a black, Hispanic, or female CEO still makes us take notice. When that becomes a part of the background of our day-to-day, I will celebrate. Then it will be the absence of the extraordinary I rejoice.

What I will acknowledge is our changing landscape. Diversity and equality look very different now, in my mid-fifties, than they did in my mid-twenties. And that, at least, is worthy of a "Woot!"

ECHO

According to Webster's, "an echo is a reflection of sound that returns repeatedly, fading with each iteration until it is gone. It repeats until it extinguishes itself and is no longer heard."

Kind of like my childhood memories, which keep bouncing around in my head, getting fainter and fainter until they're nothing more than a whisper. It may sound sad, but it isn't really. There is some kind of emotion there, but I wouldn't call it sadness. Not today, anyway. Maybe tomorrow, when I'm feeling more melodramatic.

I lived in many different places during my childhood, including three states and five countries. None of them truly felt like home, but for now, my roots are firmly planted in Dallas. If you add up the years, it's where I've spent the majority of my life. I've tried to move away, but I keep coming back, like a boomerang with a bad sense of direction. Within the city limits, I've moved too many times to count, creating a variety of stomping grounds and leaving a trail of forwarding addresses in my wake.

Today, I drove through the streets of one of those old haunts and felt the echoes of time as I passed familiar streets and hangouts. This particular neighborhood is one from my teenage years, a time when my angst was high and fashion sense was low. Fashionable or not, I still miss my OP shorts!

I saw the shadow of my fifteen-year-old self, racing down the streets on my ten-speed bike. I drove past the corner where a Taco Bueno fast-food restaurant with a pay phone outside once stood. Four streets over and several blocks away from home, I'd shovel a pocketful of quarters into that phone, talking to an older friend back in Wisconsin about how I didn't like boys, had a crush on my closest friend, and how my basketball team was calling me names I didn't understand. I was confused about all of it. She'd listen to me until I ran out of quarters, which was probably a relief for both of us. It's now a car wash, but as I went by, I caught a glimmer of the old place and a vaguely familiar kid on the phone.

Later in the morning, I passed the place where a restaurant, long since gone to a fire, used to stand. My friends and I gathered there every Saturday morning for coffee and breakfast, a ritual that was as sacred as it was necessary. The first one to wake up put out the call in a manner similar to today's phone tree, but with more yawning and grunting. Whoever answered the call then rang up the next person and so on. The dominos would fall until one by one, we were all awake— if you can call it that—and staggering into "The Vickery Feed Store."

Sometimes there would be four of us, and sometimes ten, depending on who had the worst hangover. We sat and commiserated for hours about our real-time hangovers, broken hearts, broken relationships, and new girlfriends, swearing before the breakfast table jury of peers and the never-ending coffee, "This time is for real, this is it, this is the one!" Spoiler alert: it never was.

It's all changed now and looks very different on the surface, like a bad facelift, in my nostalgic opinion. Sometimes it feels like I'm losing the anchor to that particular time in my life as my life now looks so different, like I've traded in my party shoes for sneakers. Nights out at the club have been replaced with nights in watching movies or sitting with friends. All-nighters have been replaced by a self-imposed bedtime, and after-hours parties are nonexistent, like unicorns or affordable health care. In a fit of sobering reality, and like the apology The Fonz could never spit out, I have to admit the after-hours party is g-g-gone. All gone. Long gone. Gone-gone. And for me, without hope or care to resuscitate.

I'm doing things now my younger self could never imagine, like turning my back on the corporate ladder and glass ceiling. While I can never cross the same river twice, I can look back over familiar and defining terrain, like a general surveying a battle-field.

I left the old neighborhood, comforted and warmed by nostalgia like a warm blanket wrapped around me. Echoes of memories—some clear and present, others distant and fading, like a bad radio signal—pinged inside my mind.

The fifteen-year-old longed for a time when my greatest worry was whether my hair was perfect enough, and my jeans were the right ones. The 50-something-year-old though, was content to let the echoes fade into silent gratitude.

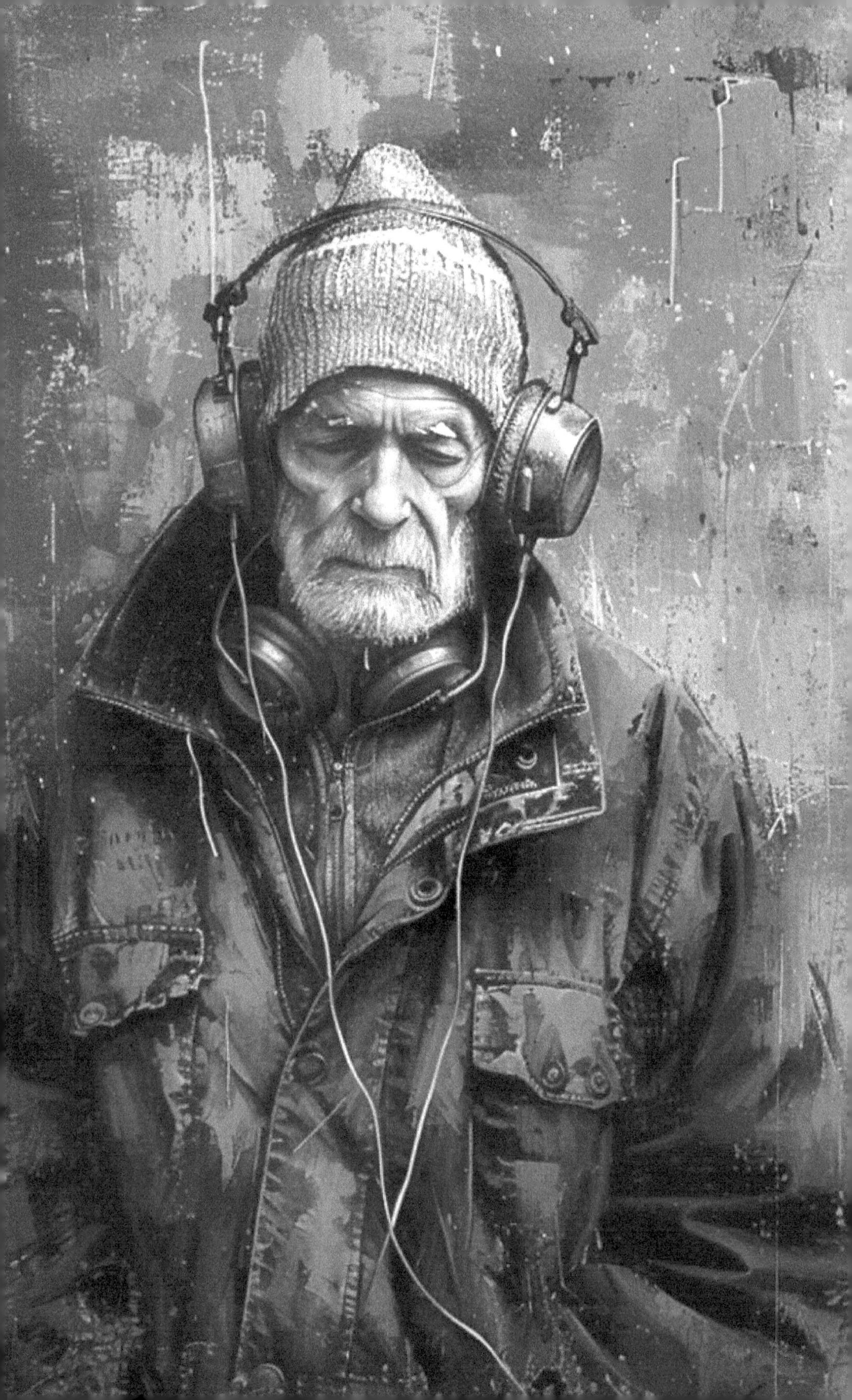

SORRY, I'M JUST HUMAN

When I hear that tired excuse, I can't help but let out a fake sneeze while muttering "*bullshit*" under my breath. With a hint of sarcasm, I think to myself, "Oh, so you're human? And here I thought you were some perfect being from another planet."

Unless we've magically teleported to a world where you're a flawless superhero, it's pretty obvious that you, like the rest of us, are human. But sure, go ahead and state the obvious while using it as a halfhearted apology. Just don't be surprised when I start seeing you as the ass you're acting like.

Recently, it feels like everyone and their cousin and brother —and let's not forget the sisters—are making mistakes, each one more impressive than the last. They'll sheepishly come back, mumbling excuses about dropping the ball, skimming over important email details, or losing crucial paperwork. And just when I think their apology couldn't be any more underwhelming, they hit me with the classic, "Sorry, I'm just human" line.

Well, thanks for the newsflash, Captain Obvious!

I'm not sure why they feel the need to add that little tidbit, instantly turning an underwhelming, mediocre apology—at best—into a truly disappointing one, but they do.

Growing up with an alcoholic mom and a dad who likely

enjoyed his fair share of drinks, I quickly learned how to handle their unpredictable moods at a young age. Part of that coping mechanism involved apologizing for their feelings, as if I somehow controlled their emotional state. I'd catch myself saying things like, "I'm sorry I made you sad," or, "I'm sorry I made you angry," even when I had no idea what was happening. But when you're ten, you might as well assume it's your fault, right?

Now, thirty to thirty-five years later (wow, time flies!), I've come to understand that a sincere apology should focus on my own actions and behavior. So, when I majorly mess up, I'll take responsibility and say something like, "I'm sorry for being insensitive," or, "I apologize for being a complete idiot," or even, "I really dropped the ball as a spouse in that situation, and I'm genuinely sorry."

We all have our flaws, and part of being human is owning up to them and apologizing when we should. An apology that actually takes accountability instead of shifting blame? Now that's refreshing!

Being human is actually extraordinary. To default to "just" being human as an excuse, minimizes our ability to correct our blunders, as if we are single cell organisms with no control over our actions. It degrades the very honor of what it is to be human. The reality is, *because* you are human is the reason you *can* do something!

But then there are those folks who think they can just casually throw out a, "Sorry, I screwed up; I'm just human," and consider the matter settled.

Reality check: That's probably one of the most emotionally immature things you can say. It's essentially admitting that you're no better than anyone else, and it absolves you of any genuine responsibility. Seems to be a trendy excuse these days, as I watch people left and right trying to evade accountability like it's a game of dodgeball. But hey, why take ownership of your actions when you can just attribute it to being human and send that apology into the abyss?

When I was a kid, I'd always try to shift the blame to my little sister whenever possible. But my parents were too smart for that. They knew she was either too young to have done whatever I was accusing her of, or she'd spill the beans quicker than I could deny it. Eventually, I'd have to own up and come clean.

Even now, there are times when my nature wants to revert back to those younger years, where I can place the blame on others.

In fact, not long ago, my boss' boss texted me, asking that I give her a call. When I get messages like this from my boss (boss with a little "b"), it gives me palpitations. So you can imagine how much more freaked out I was to get a text from the big B boss. My heart stopped, and my knees practically gave out.

I had handed off a difficult patient to one of our young, green, still wet-behind-the-ears therapists, and Big Boss wanted to know why. There was an extraordinarily long pause over the phone as I conjured up all manner of lies as to why my very senior, experienced, occupational therapist of twenty-five years self, handed off a difficult case to someone with six months of experience. No wonder this call went right past Little Boss!

I. SO. WANTED. TO. LIE. Sweet Baby Jesus, I wanted to lie. Big Boss waited patiently for my response and finally, I just confessed, I needed a break from that particular patient and his shenanigans. Big Boss was actually pretty cool about it. She said she understood, and with minimal admonishment told me not to do it again.

"Yes ma'am…Thank you, ma'am."

So, yeah, maybe you are "just human" after all—a wishy-washy, irresponsible one at that. But who am I to cast stones?

I'm just another flawed human, ducking and dodging the lame, lousy, lifeless avoidant excuses as they come at me much like whack-a mole—desperately trying to make my way through this wild world, one sarcastic remark at a time—and boy, do I have a headache!

RELEVANT

relevant /ˈrelɪv(ə)nt/ adjective

closely connected or appropriate to what is being done or considered: "What small companies need is relevant advice, not just a magic 8-ball that spits out random, nonsensical answers." "The candidate's experience is relevant to the job, but their ability to make a killer cup of coffee might just seal the deal."

appropriate to the current time, period, or circumstances; of contemporary interest: "Critics may find themselves unable to stay relevant in a changing world, but they'll always have their trusty typewriters and a healthy dose of snark." "Her films are relevant for feminists today, proving that women can kick ass on screen and behind the camera."

It is said there is nothing as certain as death and taxes. I'd like to add to that the relentless march of time. No matter how hard I try to hold on or slow down time, it just keeps ticking away, one agonizing second, one fleeting minute, one precious hour, one chaotic day at a time. Time speeding up or slowing down is really just an illusion, like the excruciatingly slow wait for the time clock to strike 5:00 and grant you sweet, sweet freedom, or the frantic race against time to clock in and avoid the wrath of your punctuality-obsessed boss.

As I get older, the incessant march of time becomes more daunting, like an approaching storm—with each boom and crack of menacing thunder serving as a reminder of my impending irrelevance. On some days, it sounds like the Jumanji drums…

Within this perpetual march is my valiant effort to remain relevant. When my niece was just a tiny, adorable terror, she grabbed my phone, and before I could snatch it back, she managed to change some of my settings. What took her mere seconds to accomplish took me a solid 30 minutes of head-scratching and frustrated muttering to undo.

Shortly after, I had a patient who was a software engineer. Recalling the epic battle my grandparents fought with setting up and programming those infernal VCRs and TVs, I asked him how we mere mortals could stay ahead of the ever-evolving tech curve. His response? "You can't." Well, thanks for the vote of confidence, buddy. I told him he wasn't exactly winning any helpful points, and in a feeble attempt to comfort me, he admitted that even as a software engineer, he was in the same rapidly sinking boat.

I feel like the desire to stay relevant is a byproduct of the Industrial Revolution, as younger, faster, and cheaper workers continue to replace older workers. Back in the day, before machines took over, we worked until our bodies gave out, not necessarily because some fresh-faced youngster stole our job and perhaps, that wasn't a good thing. Right now, I am the sum of my daily obligations and never-ending to-do list, most of which is dictated by the almighty time clock. I'm incredibly fortunate to love what I do, and if my body cooperates, I'll keep working past the age of 65 with a fair modicum of the vigor I possess now. I've already got two shiny new hips, so my future is looking brighter than it did two years ago when I was hobbling around like a rusty old robot. I'd like my relevance to be my choice, not a default of my age, able-ness, or the amount of coffee needed to get me started in the morning.

Maybe one day I'll stop giving a damn about being relevant, but for now, I find a small measure of comfort in the notion that this existential crisis is, at the very least, developmentally appropriate. After all, if I'm going to have a mid-life crisis, I might as well make sure it's age-appropriate.

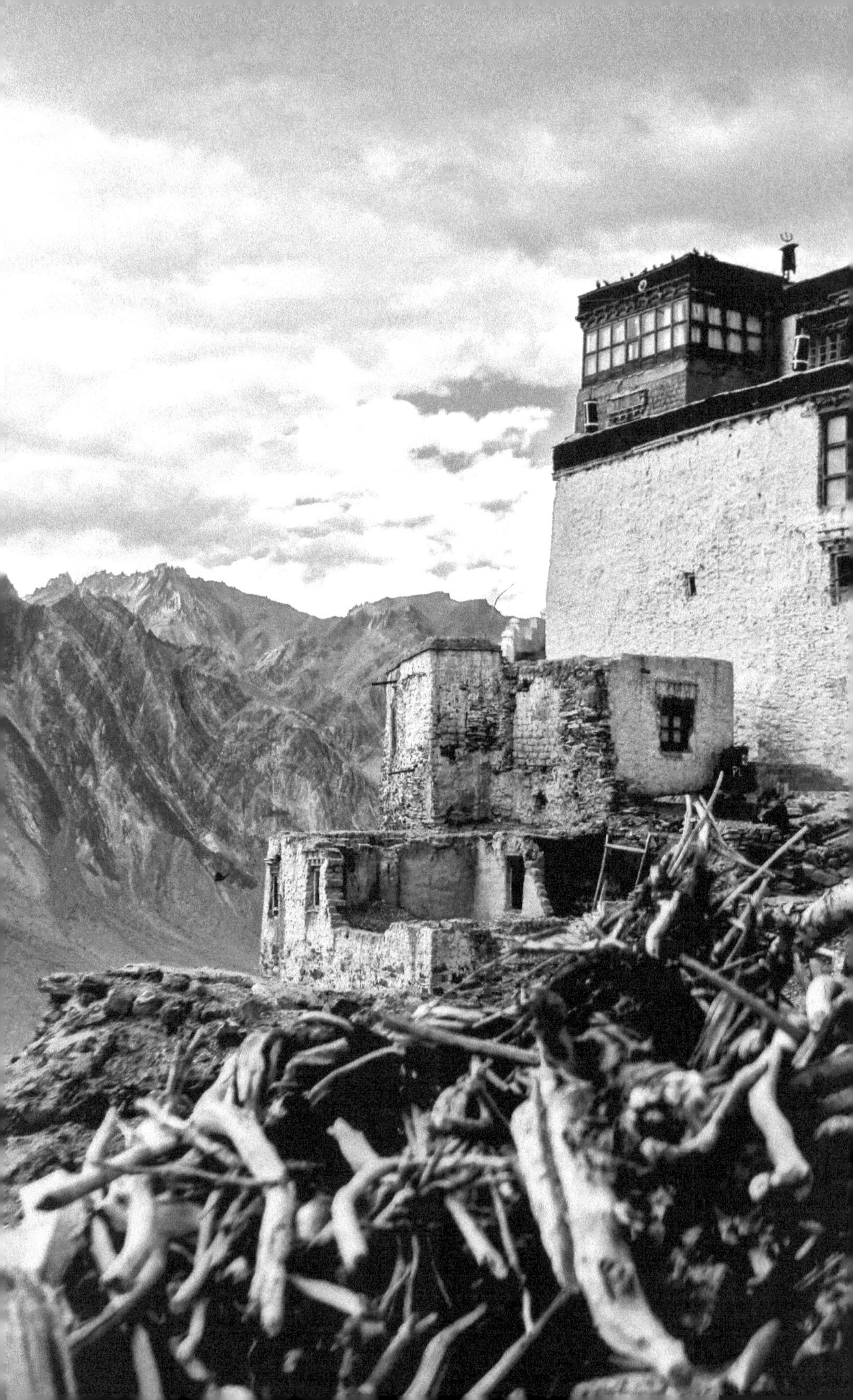

A GOOD, GOODBYE

As I've mentioned before, I was born to corporate nomads. I've lived in five different countries, three states, and been to three different high schools. It was a way of life, and though I absolutely despised it then, it turned out to be the best thing that ever happened to me. The hardest part was leaving friends behind, though, and I really, really loathed the whole goodbye thing. I mean, who actually enjoys saying goodbye?

That's why, when I graduated from the small Catholic boarding school where I spent my junior and senior year, I opted to pull-up anchor like an Irishman and slipped away without a word to anyone, not even my bestie, who loved me despite how much of an odd duck I was. Smooth, right?

I'm still amazed at how, nearly four decades later, she got past my Fort Knox-level privacy settings and managed to track me down on social media. She's been calling me a dumbass ever since for thinking no one—least of all her—would miss me.

I guess I underestimated my own charm and likability. Silly me.

It sounds cold-hearted, leaving without a goodbye, but really, my reason for doing it that way wasn't because I felt nothing for others, it's that I felt too much. The act of saying goodbye was more than I could handle. I couldn't bring myself to say it, because it meant forever, or at least a heart-wrenchingly long time. As I got older, I started saying, "see you later," whenever most people would have just said goodbye. All goodbyes were bad in my world, and they shattered my tender heart over and over again. I was like a walking, talking version of a Taylor Swift song.

That is, until that one relationship.

You know the one.

Then it became a Miley Cyrus song, and to this day, I buy my own flowers.

We were right, were good, until we weren't. Ultimately, we were such a poor match that it was more of a failed experiment than a relationship. But I think that's how poisonous relationships work. They work well initially, much like how an illusion works. They begin to disintegrate as the smoke and mirrors become more and more visible. It was toxic, emotionally draining, soul-crushing, and isolating. She took my money, managed to keep me from my friends who weren't "ours," and I swear she tried to smother my spirit like a wet blanket on a campfire. She used to tell me I cried too much. And I did. It was often at something she said or did, and that should have been my first clue early on.

But I was hooked, enticed. I was spellbound like a moth to a flame. Love makes you stupid, I guess. It made me stupid anyway.

My tender heart is one of the things I like most about myself, so I told her the day I stopped crying was the day she needed to worry. That day did come. It took everything I had to extricate myself in a final act of self-preservation, and when I left, I said goodbye.

THAT was a good goodbye.

A damn. Good. Goodbye.

HATE

I am really grappling with "hate" as a word, a descriptor, and an emotion. It's tossed about so casually these days, like confetti at a parade. My grandmother would not let us speak it or even have it as an intention. She had great disdain for it when it found its way into my vocabulary. It was definitely a word of the four letter variety to her. When I was little, she used to say it took a tiny piece of my soul every time I said it. I never got to get older with her. My grandmother died when I was ten, and I declared I hated death. In that moment I didn't care if using the word took every bit of my ten-year-old soul.

I used to have an ex who said, "whatever," all the time, with all the intonation and attitude of I-don't-give-a-shit-how-you-feel, and a somewhat blank, slightly annoyed, f-you facial expression. I asked her not to say that so much because it left me feeling emotionally kicked to the curb. What got me most was the singularly powerful TKO that came with such a mundane, generic, otherwise benign term.

So, she quit, but I still got the look, and that was just as bad, if not worse. It was like that, too, for my grandmother, with the expression we displayed when we said we hated something. Not only did we have to stop saying "hate," but we also had to "wipe that look off our faces." Apparently, "hate" has a particular facial expression, and I was guilty of wearing it often.

I am getting ready for surgery next week, and nothing is going right. My paperwork has been lost...twice. Emails and phone calls have not been returned. The different people/entities involved do not seem to be communicating with each other, and I have been hating this process with a passion. You'd think they'd be more organized. It's these interactions that have me going down the hate rabbit hole. And of course, the mental meandering leads to an endless supply of ways for me to justify using "hate" to describe a situation. Mom would say my vocabulary was lacking, that I was showing off my poor education, and of course she always said in moments like these, "I taught you much better than this."

The funny thing is, in terms of degrees of intensity, "hate" is not the strongest of this kind of emotion. According to the dictionary, "abhor," from the Latin "abhorrere"—"to shrink back in horror," is the strongest way in English to express hatred, even stronger than "loathe."

You couldn't convince my grandmother of this, though. To her, there was none more powerful than "hate." Maybe "hate" is the gateway feeling to a whole world of intensely negative emotions, like an emotional black hole. Once you go "hate," you never go back.

Marijuana, once considered the gateway drug to other illicit substances, has entered mainstream culture and has become common. "Hate," too, has entered our everyday language and is somewhat trivialized. "I hate Mondays,"..."I hate broccoli,"..."I hate my job." It's like we're all a bunch of angsty teenagers, perpetually stuck in a state of hormonal rage.

We use assigned cell phones at work that are really more of a handheld computer than a phone. In reality, they are more of a paperweight than a computer or even a phone. I find myself yelling at them, swearing at them, and saying way too often, "I hate these phones." I hear my grandmother's voice in my head, chastising me for using the word "hate," and so begins a-way-too-frequent silent argument with a voice only I know, only I hear, because today, "hate" is used so freely, like it's going out of style.

Grandma would be rolling in her grave if she knew.

I read something about the Japanese religion, Shinto, where all things have a soul, have "Kami." If this is the case, maybe my work phone would function a little better if I threw it some love. Maybe everything would work a little bit better if I threw it some love, like a sprinkle of magical fairy dust. I'll try anything at this point, even if it means having a heart-to-heart with my phone—"I love you, you piece of crap."

I'm trying, but it's not easy when the world seems to run on hate these days. I guess I'll just keep channeling my grandmother and spreading the love, one hate-free day at a time. But if that doesn't work, I'm not above giving my phone a good smack.

If we can throw the word f**k around as casually as we do nowadays, maybe the casual toss of the word "hate" no longer takes a piece of my soul.

If we can throw the word *f**k* around as casually as we do nowadays, maybe the casual toss of the word "hate" no longer takes a piece of my soul. I think now we use "hate" to mean a number of powerful feelings pegged as negative, kind of like "Kleenex" has come to mean all tissues, and "Coke" has come to represent all manner of soda, at least here in the South.

That being said, I have taken on learning different ways to express hate, or at least the whole of it, because it really takes a lot out of me.

Love fuels me; hate wears me the f**k out.

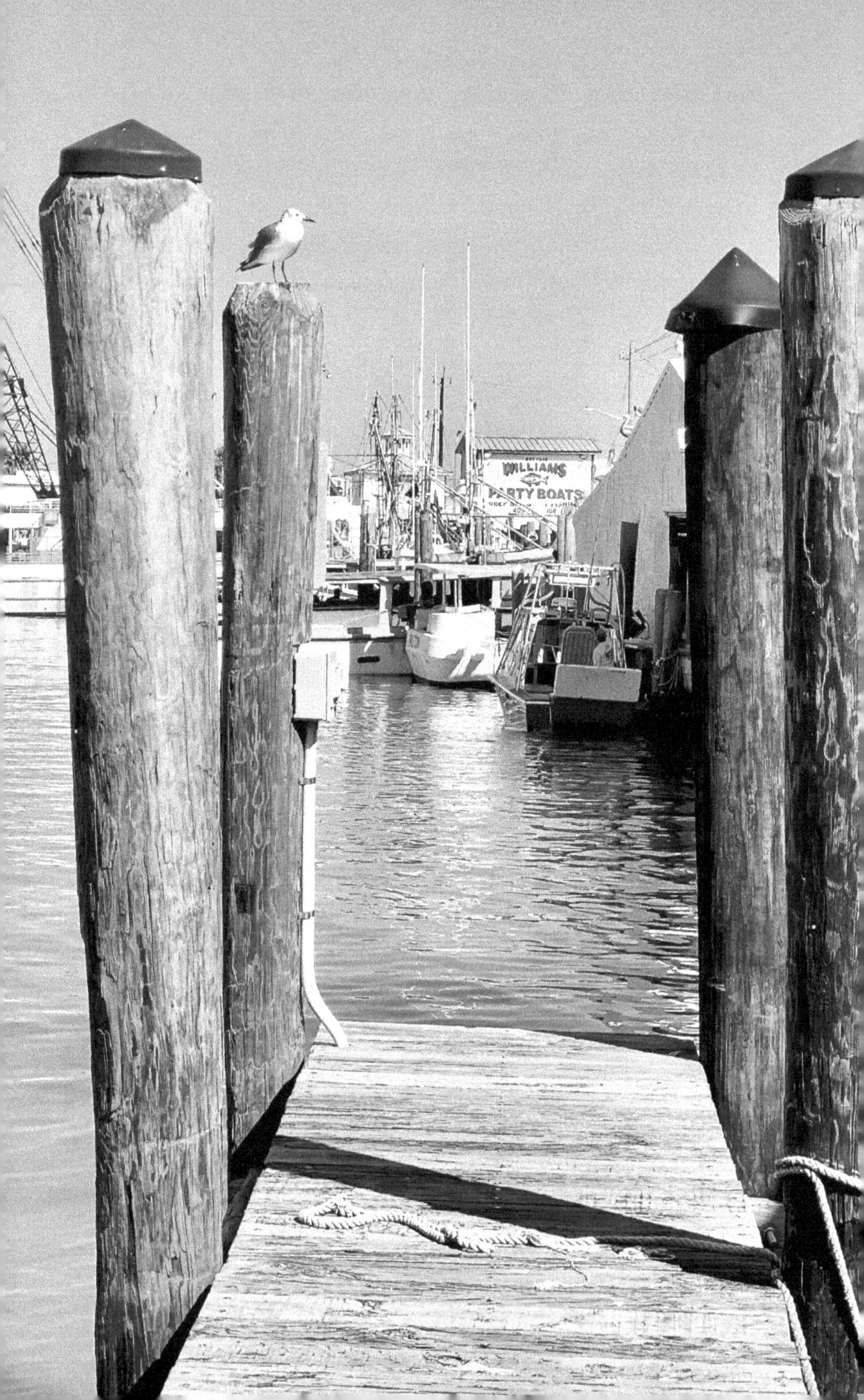

WILLIAMS
PARTY BOATS
DEEP SEA FISHING

ERIS

COVID has unleashed upon an unsuspecting world, uncertainty, chaos, and death—the likes of which has not been realized by Americans since the mid-1900s. We have lived, as a whole, ostensibly free of war, abject poverty, and disease, unlike a handful of countries around the world. Not to say we don't have our difficulties, but by and large, it's not those.

As we emerged from underneath the shroud of COVID, we entered a world of PTSD, which spanned the entirety of the COVID related spectrum. Some of us have a collective trauma response because we continued to work in the hospitals, grocery stores, delivery services, and other "essential" industries. We continued to interact with a humanity that was rather ungracefully figuring out how to manage their lives in real time amid an avalanche of change. To the opposite end, we isolated, spending the next two years without a handshake, hug, or human contact except on Zoom.

COVID is all but gone and has been since the early months of 2023. We crawled out from underneath the weight of COVID, angry and gun shy. And just when we thought it was almost over, now there's a new variant with cases rising as we enter into autumn in the northern hemisphere.

I'm not exactly sure who "they" is this time. The government? The media? The Illuminati? But the ubiquitous "they" have nicknamed this variant Eris, as in the Greek goddess of strife, discord, contention, and rivalry. She is often portrayed as the spirit of the strife of war, haunting the battlefield and delighting in human bloodshed, which seems like a perfect mascot for a pandemic that just won't quit.

I think we should have referred to COVID as Eris all along, because, like Persephone, we have all been cursed by Eris as we continue to feel something still isn't quite right, like a lingering sense of dread, or an itch you can't quite scratch.

I was thrown into an identity crisis recently when I first heard about the current COVID variant named Eris. As a healthcare worker who worked in a large public hospital during the throes of COVID, I was incensed, like a Karen demanding to speak to the manager of the pandemic. My logical side acknowledged Eris was an extremely appropriate metaphor for all of COVID, not just this particular variant. My empathetic side was indignant at the inappropriate attempt at humor, but since I do have an absurdly sick sense of humor myself, I found naming a COVID variant Eris twisted and funny, like a dad joke gone horribly wrong.

I admit, the rollercoaster of emotions I experienced had me laughing before thinking better of it and moving on to feeling insulted and angry. I can't help but wonder if the government didn't just lay down some thinly veiled culpability in that double entendre of a name before recognizing the logic of it. I do know, in the end, I laughed my ass off, giving in to my twisted sense of humor, because sometimes you just have to laugh to keep from crying.

My identity crisis continues, though, because I don't think it should be funny, but here I am, chuckling at the absurdity of it all. Maybe I should just embrace the chaos. That's not to say, I embrace COVID, but rather just the chaos, because COVID is just a small part of the chaos we call life.

CASH

Texas is one of the fastest growing states in the nation, and by extension, Dallas—though as of 2024, no longer in the top three. We have all the problems of big cities with growth spurts too huge to handle. In my opinion, our infrastructure can't handle it. The roads are too small for the population, classrooms are over-stuffed, and teachers are in short supply. Last, but by no means least, the cost of housing is beyond the reach of most.

Speaking of the meteoric cost of housing in Dallas, our homeless population is reaching new heights as well. Homelessness is a very complex and multilayered labyrinth of a problem. One layer is the lack of mental health available in general, and especially in Texas. When it comes to taking care of our mentally ill, Texas scores are abysmal. Many of these folks end up homeless as well. According to Forbes, we are the number one worst state for mental health. On the flip side, we have one of the lowest needs for mental health. I say ostensibly at least.

Homelessness is a topic that will take me on a tangent in a whisper of a second, and one in which I feel so utterly helpless. I am that kid that brought home every stray animal and person I befriended, every playground underdog. At ten, I was taller and bigger than all of the boys, so I became the self-proclaimed schoolyard bouncer—the anti-bully bully you could say. I wanted to rescue all the strays and misfits. The two and four-legged variety. To my tender heart, it is bitterly painful not to be able to help, so the enormity of homelessness is unimaginable to me.

Yesterday, I came across a young man who was probably homeless. He popped a squat on the curb of a busy street corner, head down, flicking a piece of paper I assumed was his sign asking for money. I looked at him and gave a sheepish, sad smile, hoping to convey my apology for having no money. I also wanted to make sure I saw him. I did not want to be one of the countless people driving by that either doesn't see, or worse, ignores, homeless folks. Then, in a whisper of a second, I began counting my blessings.

Positive I didn't have any cash on me, as I seldom do these days, I didn't consider taking my wallet out. Even the vending machines at work will take a card. That little voice in my head urged me to look anyway, and it turns out I had two dollars.

By now, the traffic had inched past him, and I was second in line at the stop light, in the middle lane. I tap, tap, tapped my horn, and he came running up. He skulked a toothless, twitchy smile through an overgrown beard. He never said a word, and though my knee-jerk thought was he was a junkie, I imagined his smile was more a "thank you" at being acknowledged than because he was two dollars closer to his next fix.

Admittedly, he very well could be mentally ill where the facial twitches are a side effect of psych meds, and overall poor hygiene is a result of the mental illness as well.

I didn't know what's so for him, but I am open to supporting the truth of a fellow human being.

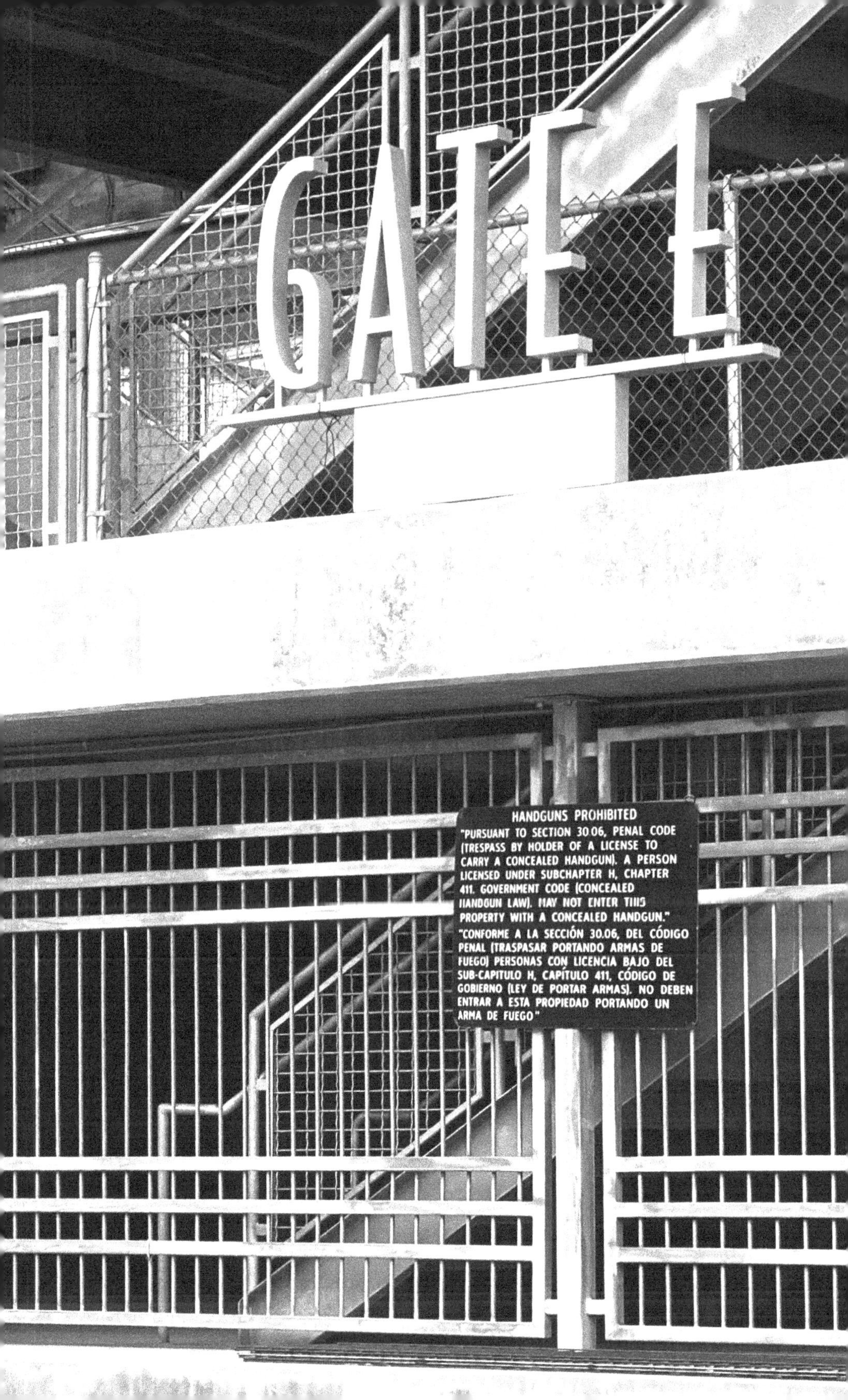

GATE E
HANDGUNS PROHIBITED
"PURSUANT TO SECTION 30.06, PENAL CODE
(TRESPASS BY HOLDER OF A LICENSE TO
CARRY A CONCEALED HANDGUN). A PERSON
LICENSED UNDER SUBCHAPTER H, CHAPTER
411. GOVERNMENT CODE (CONCEALED
HANDGUN LAW). MAY NOT ENTER THIS
PROPERTY WITH A CONCEALED HANDGUN."
"CONFORME A LA SECCIÓN 30.06, DEL CÓDIGO
PENAL (TRASPASAR PORTANDO ARMAS DE
FUEGO) PERSONAS CON LICENCIA BAJO DEL
SUB-CAPITULO H, CAPÍTULO 411, CÓDIGO DE
GOBIERNO (LEY DE PORTAR ARMAS). NO DEBEN
ENTRAR A ESTA PROPIEDAD PORTANDO UN
ARMA DE FUEGO"

DOG GONE IT

I got my very own first dog when I was twenty-one—a purebred black lab I named Abby. Her imperfect features disqualified her from being a show dog, but that was ok...I wasn't going to show her anyway. I was imperfect for showing too, so we were a perfect pair, and for the next sixteen years, we grew up together, like two peas in a slightly dysfunctional pod.

Our first place—a tiny apartment with a community pool and not much more—was filled to the brim with happy memories of Abby and me. People griped, claiming I was no better than a prison guard keeping this poor ball of energy in such squashed living conditions, but Abby didn't care. We spent hours each day visiting dog parks and playing fetch with balls and frisbees, and by the time we got home, my little black Energizer Bunny was completely on empty, and would spend the next few hours lazily napping on the couch or in her doggie bed.

What she did mind, however, was the pool. She hated it when I swam! Dogs weren't allowed at the pool, but sometimes I'd sneak her in when no one else was around. She'd nervously pace back and forth at the water's edge until she couldn't stand it anymore. She'd whimper and whine before finally jumping in. Grabbing my wrist, she'd drag me to the side of the pool, safe and sound. She was a Labrador Retriever, after all; it was in her DNA to retrieve me!

When we moved into our first "real" home, I thought for sure that Abby was going to love the big backyard. But she didn't. I'd put her out and close the glass paneled door, only to look back and find her staring at me, like, "You're not coming too?'

She was the only constant in my life then. During those years with Abby, we moved so many times, I lost count. She was such a trooper, especially during our move to Portland, OR. I loaded her up with the rest of my prized possessions and drove halfway across the country. She had to pee more than I did, so we stopped frequently. Apparently, her bladder was the size of a peanut

Our first day on the road, we drove straight through from Dallas, TX to Laramie, WY. Exhausted from the umpteen hours in the car, we happened upon a sweet little Mom & Pop motel. I snuck her in the room, where she promptly plopped on the bed, claiming it as her own. The trip must've completely worn her out though, because in the morning, we woke to a puddle of pee where she had slept.

Her puppy dog eyes glossed with embarrassment and broke this momma's heart. I also felt bad for housekeeping, so in an effort to camouflage the accident, I placed a glass on the bed in the middle of the puddle, and hoped they would assume I spilled water there instead. Feeling guilty, I left a small tip on the dresser as well, and before the sun could hint at rising, Abby and I made our departure. It was our little secret.

Abby was there for everything. She was my constant companion through thick and thin. Anytime a love interest became more than a passing curiosity, or a relationship of mine crashed and burned, or even when my parents' relationship crashed and burned, Abby was there. She was even there when I had to say goodbye to my mom, and Abby helped carry me through the grief of losing a parent.

She was one tough cookie, that's for sure! Not only did she

have to have the end of her tail amputated because of an infected hot spot, but she tore the tip of her ear, making it slightly shorter than the other. It didn't matter though, it only added to her adorableness, giving her a jaunty, lopsided look.

We spent a good amount of time taking trips to the vet. Sometimes for emergencies, like when she ate therapy putty, and again after downing a whole BIG bag of M&M's. Other times it was for more serious things, like when she tore her left ACL while playing fetch. The vet told us at that visit she was too old for surgery, but two years later, she tore the other ACL, yet again while playing fetch, and this time the vet went ahead with surgery.

After that, fetch had to be played a little differently. I wanted her to still feel like she was fetching, but didn't want her getting hurt, so I gently lobbed the ball to her and made the game easier.

While still in Oregon, Abby started to slow down tremendously. I didn't think too much of it until one day, when she got weirdly sick and was acting abnormal. I walked into the room and stopped abruptly. Abby had slowly made her way to the corner of the house, and with her head lowered, she sat facing the wall. I knew something was off...way off. So I scooped her up and rushed to the vet yet again.

It was a freakishly beautiful day in Portland for February. Normally, the dark skies were covered in heavy gray clouds that soaked the ground with cold rain. But instead, the sun shined warm and bright. Looking back, I suppose the weather should've given me hope that everything was going to be ok, but it didn't.

After what felt like forever, the vet delivered the news—cancer. I needed to be sure though, so I requested more tests. They shaved Abby's front legs to put in IVs and loaded her up with fluids. When she came bounding into the room where I waited, she looked mostly normal. Unfortunately, looks are deceiving, and the vet confirmed that she had cancer, and that the kindest thing I could do for her, was to let her go.

The vet gazed out of the window at the blue skies, then suggested, "If you want, you can take her to the park one last time. It's a beautiful day; you could say goodbye with a final game of fetch, maybe?"

I just shook my head. I knew if I took her out of that office, I wouldn't have the strength to bring her back. So instead, I sat on the floor, hugging her and crying into her dark fur. The vet even sat by my side. Abby, the ever faithful companion, lovingly licked my face, doing her best to comfort me, even in her final moments.

I had to grow up some more that day, but this time, I was forced to do it without her.

Abby stole my heart, and never gave it back.

A few days later, invited by friends, I went to a fundraising concert in an old church. The woman performing was Joan Armatrading. Still heavy with grief, I snuck in late and sat in the back, by myself, afraid my grief was contagious. She strummed the guitar as she sang an old kids' song about a dog named Blue. I had only ever paid attention to the first few lines of the song, but as her voice carried over the crowd, the rest of the lyrics pummeled in my chest and wrung out fresh agony.

> Now, Old Blue died and he died so hard
> Made a big dent in my back-yard
> Dug his grave with a silver spade
> Lowered him down with a link of chain
> Ev-er-y link I did call his name...
> Singing "Here...old...Blue-ue...
> "Good dog you."

At that moment, I promised myself the next dog I got, I'd name Blue, and I kept that promise…

Two years later, I got a half yellow lab, half golden retriever mix. She moved with me back to Texas and was my new lifeboat. Yet again, I had a constant companion to help me through one failed relationship after another. When Blue was eight, I asked about a doggie DNR. The vet assured me that while it's a good idea, Blue was nowhere near ready for that, like she was some kind of canine superhero, immune to the ravages of time.

At twelve, I started dragging her into the vet for geriatric wellness checks every six months. She loved car rides, but as soon as she saw the vet's office, she'd hide on the passenger-side floorboard, desperately trying to disappear into the carpet. As I made my way to the other side of the car, she went opposite of wherever I went, forcing me to eventually strong-arm her out, like a cop wrangling a reluctant suspect.

At sixteen, her body was failing, and it was failing fast. Sadly, her mind failed faster. She often got lost if she wandered to the other side of the bed or into the bathroom. After a few minutes, I'd realize she wasn't where she was supposed to be, and I'd go find her, like a sad, one-sided game of hide-and-seek.

I loved Blue, and it broke my heart to see her deteriorate so quickly. One day, I sat with her, and as I stroked her head, I gave her permission to go, and as much as it hurt, I promised I would be okay without her. Blue was stubborn, though, and wouldn't give up. Months later, my once healthy seventy-five pound, robust ball chaser withered to a mere fifty pounds. People thought I was starving her, like I was some kind of monster. I ended up having to get a harness for her because her legs would go out so often underneath her. Everytime they buckled, I'd grab the harness and lift her like a furry little forklift.

I hated being on the outside looking in. I wasn't sure

exactly what Blue was going through—what kind of quality of life she had—but I knew she was fading. A year prior to her weird behavior, the vet had told me she was ready for the doggie DNR, so I knew the end was close. I wasn't trying to keep her alive longer, I just wanted to keep her comfortable for as long as she chose to stay with me.

Once more, I found myself face to face with one of the most agonizing decisions I would have to make.

Like Abby, Blue had traveled the country with me and protected my heart. We played ball, tug, and snuggled, and she was my constant companion. She, too, stole my heart, the little bit that grew back anyway. Saying goodbye to her was just as hard as saying goodbye to Abby, and left me broken in pieces once more.

I once had a dog, a dog named Blue. Don't you wish you had one, too?

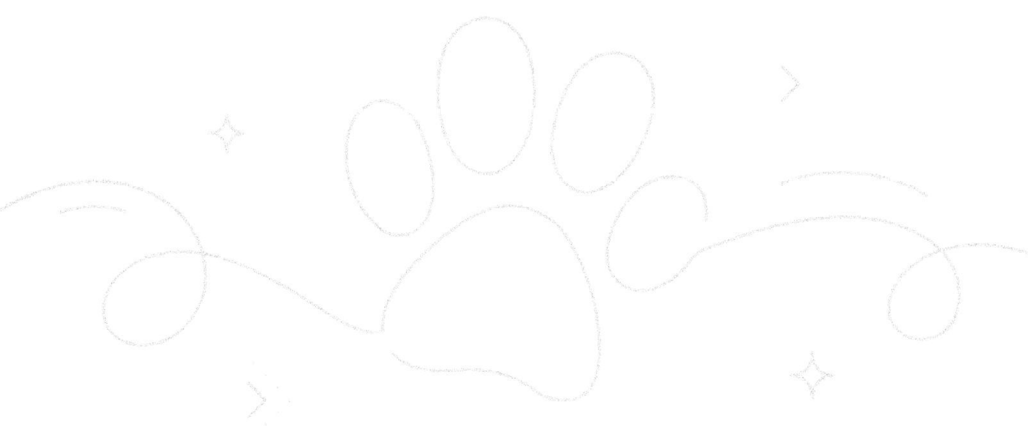

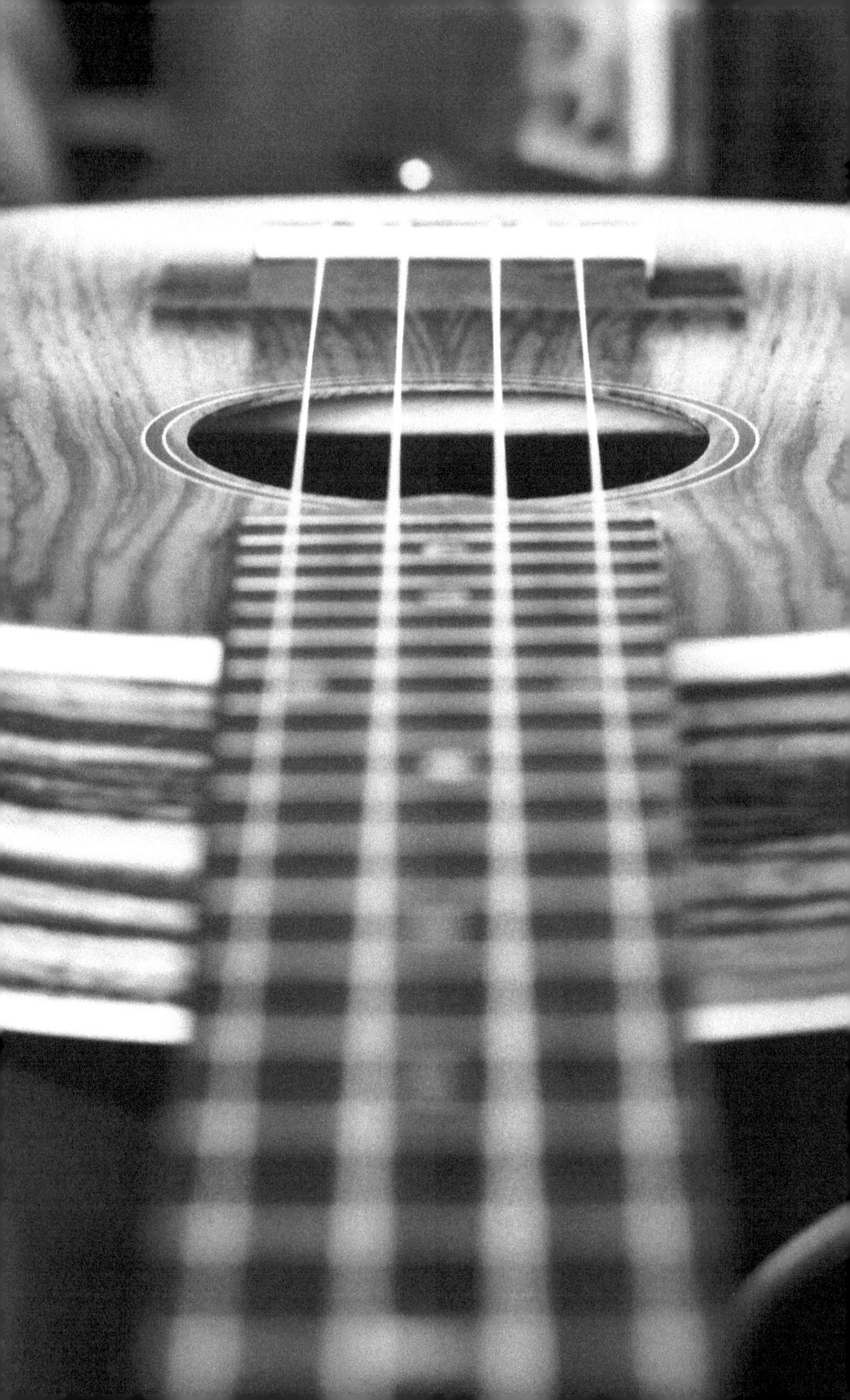

HAPLESS

Twelve months, fifty-two weeks, three hundred and sixty-five days, or eight thousand, seven hundred and sixty hours. It all adds up to one thing, and they are piling up like the dust bunnies under my bed or the complaints in my inbox.

What do dust bunnies, complaints, and a year have in common? Sounds like the beginning of a bad joke! Dust bunnies—like complaints and years—accumulate, at first unnoticed, and then hijack my attention until I do something about them.

This past week, I had a birthday. Not a milestone birthday, thank God! Just a birthday, but it was another trip around the sun as *they* say. *They*? Who exactly is *they*? I have actually always wondered who *they* is? But we'll save that for another time, another essay.

I don't mind birthdays. I rather enjoy the celebrations. But I don't enjoy the growth spurts that seem to tag along. When I was a teenager, my growth spurts were so painful, I was frequently in tears. Like grit-your-teeth-try-not-cuss-and-call-the-tears-sweat kind of pain. This was also before Motrin, so not much in the way of pain relief either. At ten, the growth was less "spurt" and more "surge," which stretched my ligaments and tendons so much to the point they could not hold my knee in place. Anytime I came close to ninety degrees, it dislocated.

I was in a straight leg plaster cast for six weeks. I had to do five hundred leg lifts a day—doctor's orders—just to keep the damn thing up or I'd have to wear "cast suspenders." A cast was cool. Cast suspenders were not. But I digress.

This year's birthday will go down as the one I declared "Time to take care of me, and not deal with other people's toxic traits while dealing with my own."

It all began with birthday plans that unraveled like a cheap bathing suit, revealing the naked truth and virgin vulnerability underneath that very quickly got burned.

A friend, knowing I'd understand, bailed on my birthday weekend plans because she got a chance to go on a cruise for free. I was happy for her, and I *did* understand, but there was still a small piece of my heart that felt like she could be bought for the cost of a ride on a damn boat. Turned out the cruise was the following month, but instead of resuming our plans, she said yes to babysitting. And again, although I understood, it still felt like B.S.-two, Anne-zero.

Since our friend wasn't coming, Kris assumed all weekend plans were off, and scheduled work. She figured I'd understand because she is building her business. Yeah, I did understand, AND I was pissed. You know what they say…

THEY…really, who the f**k is *they*?

Anyway, you know what *they* say about people who assume things, right?* Go ahead and apply it here, because I thought she was an ass at that moment, and I later made an ass out of myself.

I worked overtime and flexed a shift to get Sunday off, but it all came tumbling down around me like a house of cards, and I was left with a miserable game of fifty-two pick up.

I. WAS. NOT. HAPPY. And kept recounting the losses over and over:

1. A friend cancels our weekend birthday plans to go on a free cruise. *Oof!*

2. Turns out the free cruise is next month, and instead of resuming the plans, she stays home to babysit her grandson on a weekend she was not supposed to be home anyway. *Ouch!*

3. Kris schedules work on Sunday, assuming I'd go back to work myself since said friend was not coming. *Aaaarrggh! What the hell?*

What was really not a big deal, quickly became huge. Kris could not deal with my sadness at having my plans crumble, and we ended up arguing all weekend. I talked to another friend who told me to stop being dramatic. The one or two other conversations I tried went similarly, and I eventually gave up in a fizzle of exasperation.

Damn…if I didn't have bad luck, I'd have no luck.

Holy, hapless, hell! Everyone? All at the same time! And not one person understood I was just *sad.* They all spoke to the hyper-adult I usually am in a suck-it-up-and-put-on-your-big-girl-panties manner. But that's not who was sad. The little girl inside me was sad, and the more they spoke, the bigger my sadness became.

So, the adult in me told them all to f**k off, and that I quit. I quit adulting for a week. If no one else was going to listen to me, then I was.

None of these folks are bad or mean. No one can do or say the right thing at the right time, all the time, and as I begged outside myself for someone to listen, it forced me to get quiet and listen to myself instead. Not to the list of monotonous complaints that were piling up, but to the strength that is generated *by me* and not *outside of me.*

Here is what "we"—my little girl and I—figured out, or rather, what she taught me and I learned: The gift I so wanted but never got, is the gift of being heard. Even if it is me hearing my inner little girl.

I got hijacked this past weekend. I think I'm back on track and am looking for a therapist to learn better communication skills. But, much to the dismay of my Mormon editors, Catholic mother, very Catholic Grandmother, and Jewish grandmother on my grandfather's side, I'm never giving up the use of my favorite go-to phrase, "*F**k off.*"

*Just in case you don't know, there is a saying about assuming things that goes like this: When you "ass/u/me," it makes an *ass* out of *u* and *me*.

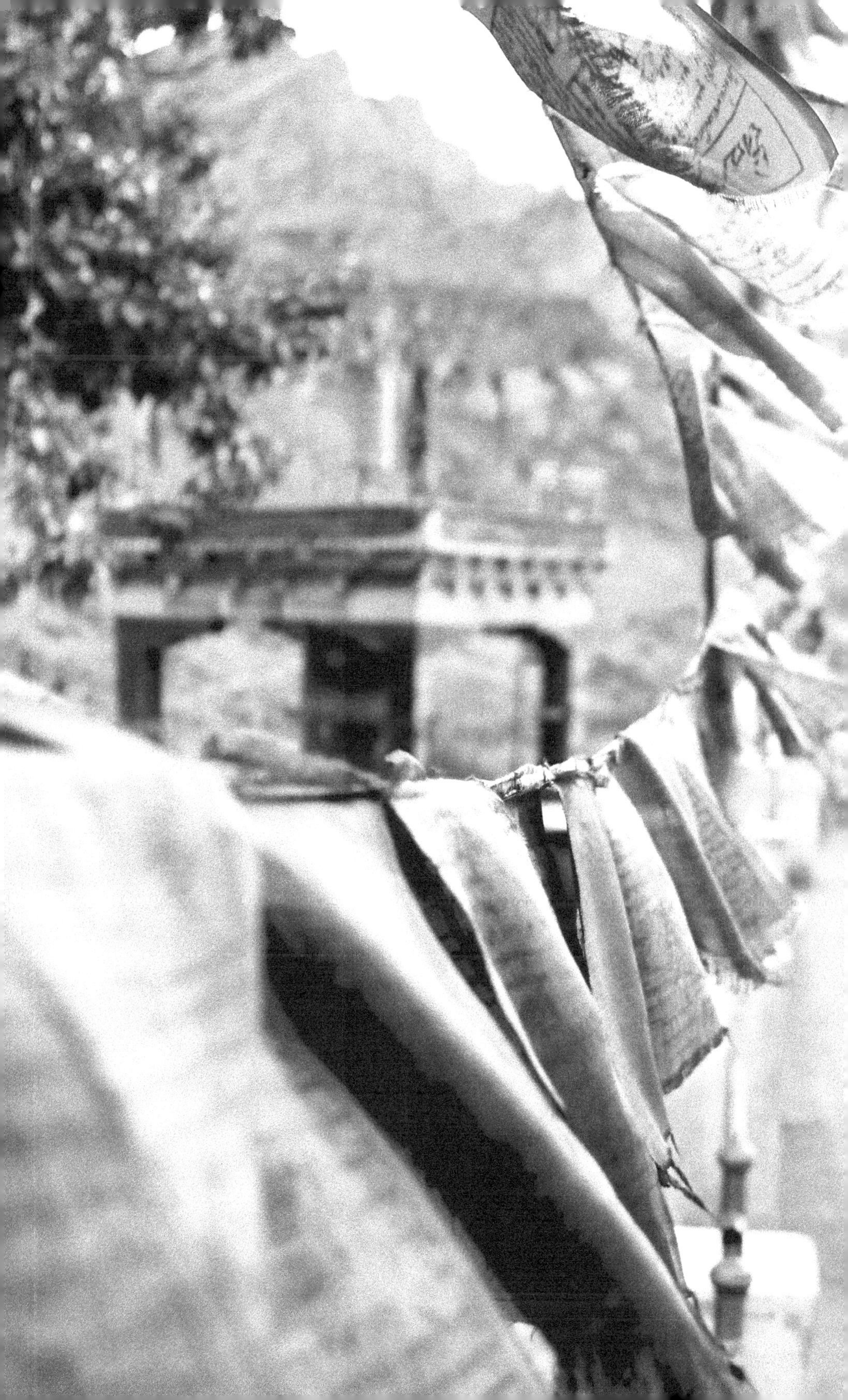

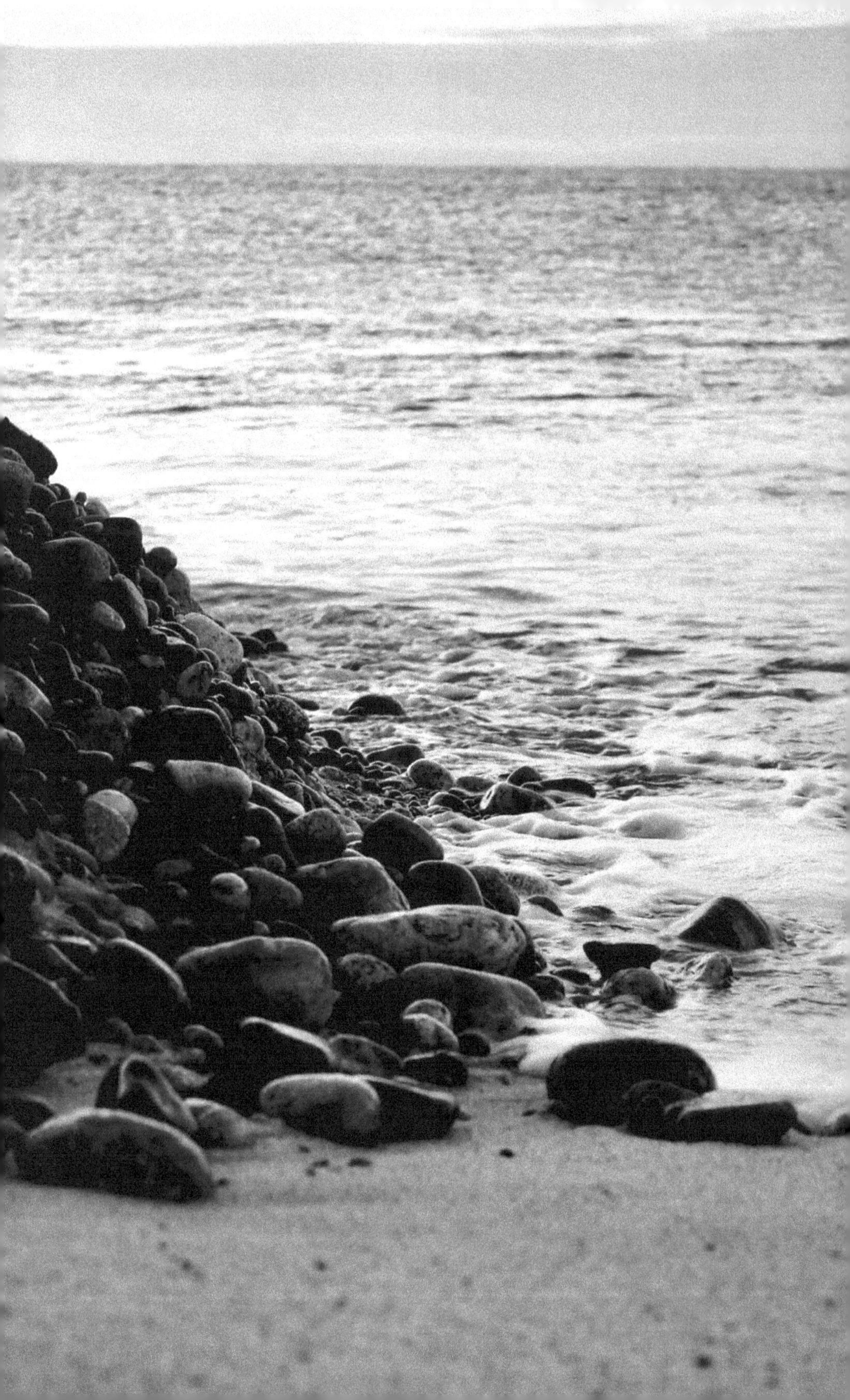

THANK YOU

I've been told I don't need a thank you page because my book is not the kind to become a bestseller. On the off chance it becomes a one-hit wonder, and the off, off chance I become a some-what-famous author, there are a handful of folks that have earned my heartfelt and eternal thanks.

It's a short list, because for so long, no one knew I could write, and at the very top is Kris—my heart, my forever. She listened to countless versions and offered only joyous support.

Next is my closest friend, Michael Simmons. He died before he could see this come to fruition, but knew I was breathing life into it. He was my biggest cheerleader, and we would philoso-phize for hours over many of the topics. He'd say, "You're really good, you know." I still have a hard time believing him.

To my coach, Kym Dolcimascolo—it took five years of pok-ing, nudging, and prodding, then it was just a matter of months when I bit the bullet. Love you big!

Thank you, Valerie Andrew! There needs to be a heart icon on a keyboard just for you. You gave me a launch pad from which to leap where one never existed. I will love you forever.

My brother-in-law, Paul, has a very special place in my heart. Of all the people that said they wanted to read what I wrote, he is one of a handful who actually did.

Mia Marks read it anywhere she could and despite being 30 years my junior, encouraged me more than she knows.

And my sister who always, always, always, believes in me. You win.

PHOTOS

Cover: **PRAYER FLAGS** In 2017 I took a trip to a tiny village in the Indian Himalaya's were exiled Tibetans and the Dali Lama fled. There were prayer flags everywhere that somehow contributed to the surroundings in a way much bigger than just their collective strings and color.

Back Cover: **DEEP IN THE HIMALAYAS** In 2017 I went to Northern India to volunteer at a tiny village hospital. The views and scenery were truly divine

Title Page: **WYOMING OPEN ROAD** This was snapped driving through Wyoming on our way to Montana. What makes this pic is the haze which is smoke from one of the worst forest fire seasons in Montana's history.

Page 1: **MENACE** I turned to ai to create an image to depict the little demons in us all that hijack our common sense. Once I got past some seriously wicked, satanic-looking images, I got this guy which much more aptly depicts a momentary lapse in judgement, a frontal lobe override vs, going postal, which the other images suggested.

Page 4: **SAN JUAN, PR** The Streets of old San Juan

Page 8: **BEACH Nº 1, STORMY SEAS IN CABO** The not peaceful Pacific off the coast of Mexico, after a storm. The ocean in Cabo is beautiful and when a storm rolls in, it is equally dangerous.

Page 14: **BOYS IN THE BAND** While in NOLA I wandered aimless around the city, into the corner's and back alleys when I came across this street band warming up.

Page 21: **ROAD LESS TRAVELED** A beautiful spring day is always a good reason for a photograph.

     FUMBLES, STUMBLES, AND GRUMBLES

Page 25: **MISIÓN DE NUESTRA SEÑORA DEL PILAR, TODO SANTOS, MÉXICO** I was fortunate enough to get this shot without the distraction of people to complicate the simplicity that is this beautiful little church in Todo Santos Mexico.

Page 34: **OLD FASHIONED TROLLEY** I was awake at 0600 on my vacation in San Francisco and captured the inside of this refurbished, repurposed trolley car before rush hour began.

Page 38: **DEEP IN THE HIMALAYAS** In 2017 I went to Northern India to volunteer at a tiny village hospital. The views and scenery were truly divine

Page 42: **FOUR MINUTES** This an AI rendering of my idea of collective time. It's different and the same for all of us.

Page 50: **M&M'S TIMES SQUARE, NY** Like good little tourists, we did a double decker bus tour of the highlights of NYC and it included this gem.

Page 55: **WYOMING SUNSET** We were driving to Montana, and I caught the sun as it slipped behind the mountains.

Page 56: **TIMES SQUARE** Sometimes a photo does not tell the whole story. There is a grittiness to Times Square that just isn't captured here.

Page 60: **BLUEBONNETS AND SCHOOL BUS** The perennial Texas Bluebonnet is a harbinger of school's end, rising temps, and all manner of family photos in the fields of our state flower. Any Texas photo collection is incomplete without a shot of the ubiquitous bluebonnet.

Page 64: **ZEEDIJK STREET, AMSTERDAM** Zeedijk Street is one of the oldest streets in Amsterdam

Page 68: **MIDTOWN SOUND** Some things never change and over the years, music has come to be one of those things no matter how old, the genre, or how it's played

Page 72: **OLD CHURCH** San Juan, Puerto Rico

Page 78: **THUNDERBIRD** I came across this old classic and had to grab a photo. It's not a Silver Thunderbird, but worthy of a song nonetheless.

Page 82: **MIX TAPE** I went to the internet and then to AI to find an image for this photo. In the end, I set up and made my own. There was nothing I found that came close to the experience of making a mix tape, of which I made many over the years. It was a rite of passage of sorts—a very cryptic teenage diary and became a competition for the coolest mixtape.

Page 86: **FAIRVIEW ST., HOUSTON TX** There is nothing like getting lucky. The stage was set for this to be a great shot. The passing storms made the roads wet and shining, the restaurants were all lit up and dark colored vehicles all in a row added nice contrast to the bright lights. Imagine my surprise when I got the prints back and saw I was photo bombed by the pick-up in motion. It's a much better shot for it!

Page 90: **MOSQUITO FLEET** The Mosquito Fleet is the name of Galveston Islands' very own shrimping fleet.

Page 93: **DADDY'S SHOES** When she was little, my niece was always clomping around in father's shoes. This time we caught a picture.

Page 94: **OBX BEACH** This is a shot of the beach perfection that is The Outer Banks

Page 98: **REFLECTIONS** The scenery in the Himalayas is breathtaking but when you're there for two weeks it becomes ordinary so I looked for new ways to capture that beauty.

Page 102: **THE STAR DRUGSTORE** is a Galveston icon. It is an old fashioned drug store/soda fountain that is more restaurant and kitch these days. It has withstood the test of time

Page 108: **MORNING FOG** This was taken as I headed out for work.

Page 117: **DOOR 9 ¾** New Orleans is a magical town and walking about I came across this door which has SO much going on. It begged for a photograph.

Page 120: **SAN JUAN, PR** The Streets of old San Juan

Page 126: **FLOWERS** Just everyday flowers that makes an ordinary day, extraordinary.

Page 130: **KA'AN LUUM LAGOON, MEXICO** This is a very shallow body of water, where lies in the middle a center so deep you have to be a registered scuba diver to go out there—hense, the float line and signage just beyond the pier.

Page 138: **OLD HARVESTER INTERNATIONAL TRUCK** This is an old Harvester International truck left to return to nature on the big island of Hawaii

Page 143: **STAIRWAY TO HEAVEN** I say heaven because this is in Glacier National Park, which really is a little bit of heaven on earth

Page 144: **TOM MOORE BUILDING, HOT SPRINGS, AR** I also love old buildings and when I saw the reflection catch a hint of that old signage, I was head over heels!

Page 156: **JUST HUMAN** Again, I went to the internet and then to AI to come up with an image to visually reprent the feeling of irrelevant. I really wanted a picture of an old beat up Sony Walkman and each descriptor I put into the software lead me further and further from that particular image utilizing it produced this image. There is so much about this that is irrelevant today and very realistic, metaphorical and sad kinda way.

Page 164: **STONGDEY MONASTERY** This is a Buddhist monastery in Zanskar, India, built in 1052 C.E.

Page 170: **BAY SIDE** Galveston Bay is where the infamous "mosquito fleet" resides—Galveston's own shrimping fleet.

Page 175: **THE COTTON BOWL** A Texas icon

Page 182: **UKULELE** As the saying goes, when in Rome or in this case Hawaii. We bought a Ukulele and learned a bit of the craft in a crash lesson.

Page 187: **PRAYER FLAGS** In 2017 I took a trip to a tiny village in the Indian Himalaya's were exiled Tibetans and the Dali Lama fled. There were prayer flags everywhere that somehow contributed to the surroundings in a way much bigger than just their collective strings and color.

Page 188: **BEACH Nº 3** Just another beautiful beach in Cancun

Page 195: **NEW WTC** This is an image of The New World Trade Center in NYC. While it's beautiful and a work of art in its own rite, it stands on hallowed ground as an eternal reminder and shoulders the burden of a city, country, and generation.

Page 196: **DEEP IN THE HIMALAYAS** When in the small Buddhist village in Northern India, the roads were often nonexistent. What looks like a babbling brook in this photo, was our road.

Page 198: **WHITE STALLION RANCH,** outside of Tucson AZ has rescued a number of horses and this is just one

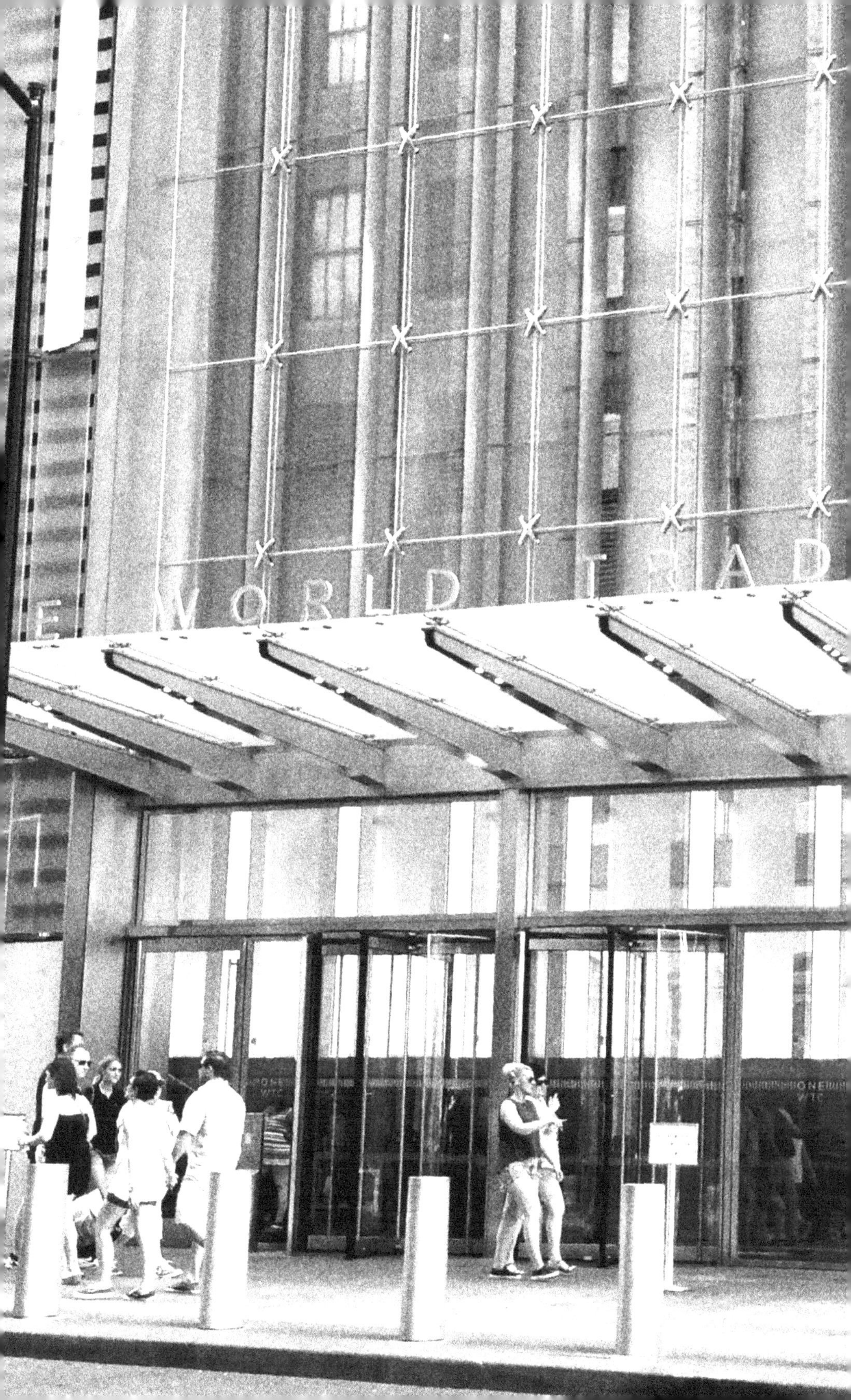
E WORLD TRAD

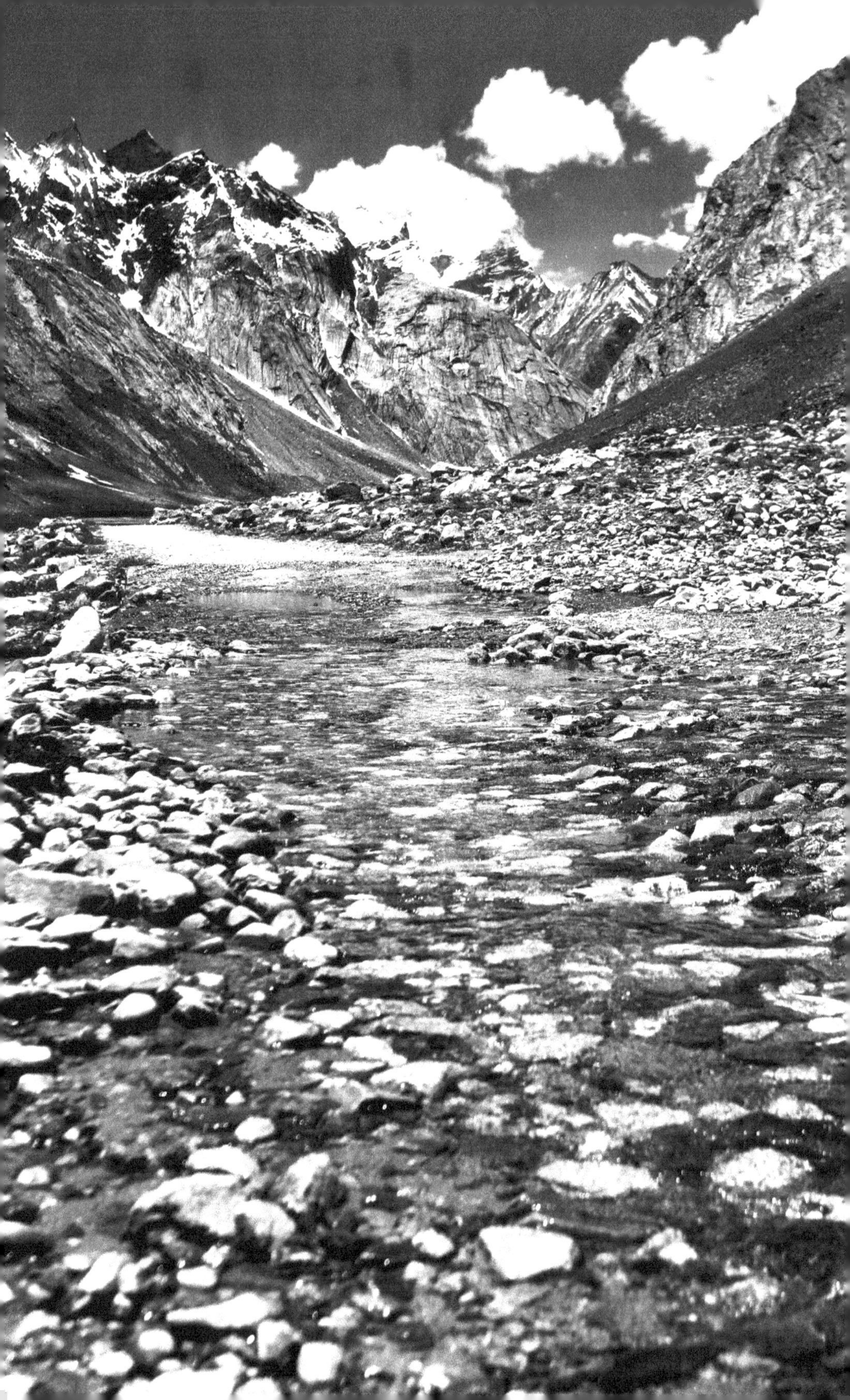

ANNE VALENTINE

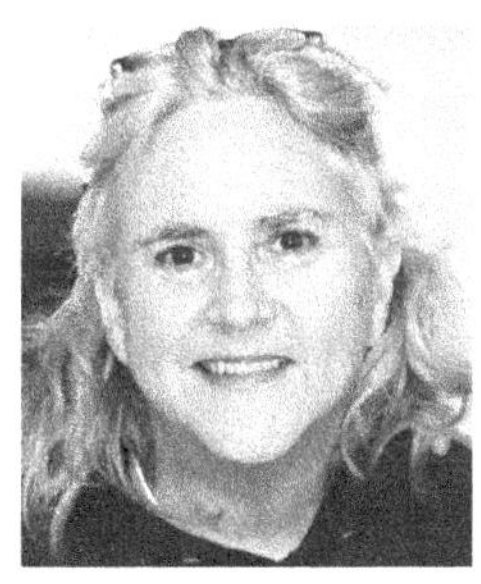

I am a Gen X daughter of a corporate executive and housewife. I grew up in our midwestern home knowing I was college bound. My parents threatened me with college or I'd be kicked out of the house at 18. Since I was a good little rule follower with an attitude problem, I went to school and made it as unconventional as possible.

I have been an Occupational Therapist for the last 32 years and somewhere along the way began writing. Feeling the need to get things out of my head and out of my way, I wrote them down-all the things I wondered about, thought about, worried about.

The few people I shared these musings with said they were good, good enough to write a book. Eventually I put those thoughts together with some of my photographs and did just that.

I am still an occupational therapist and now, an incidental author.

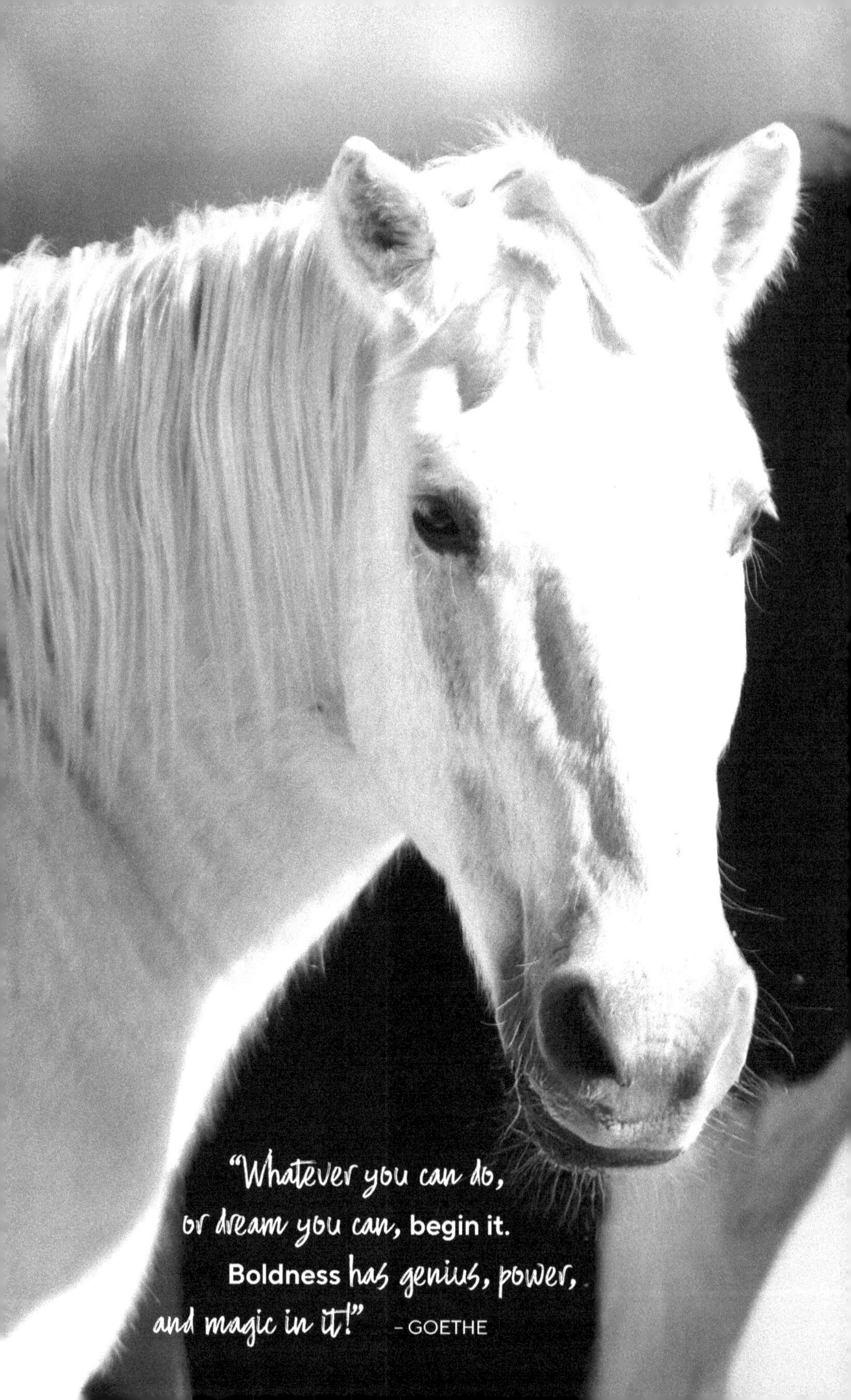

"Whatever you can do,
or dream you can, begin it.
Boldness has genius, power,
and magic in it!" – GOETHE

* 9 7 9 8 8 9 4 5 4 0 8 7 0 *